GRAN CANARIA

SPIRALGUIDE

AA Publishing

Contents

Written by Tony Kelly
Revised and updated by Jackie Staddon and Hilary Weston

Revision managed by Bookwork Creative Associates
Series Editor Karen Rigden
Series Designer Catherine Murray

Published by AA Publishing, a trading name of AA Media Limited,
whose registered office is Fanum House, Basing View, Basingstoke,
Hampshire, RG21 4EA. Registered number 06112600.

ISBN: 978-0-7495-6242-7

The contents of this publication are believed correct at the time
of printing. Nevertheless, AA Publishing accept no responsibility
for errors, omissions or changes in the details given, or for the
consequences of reader's reliance on this information. This does
not affect your statutory rights. Assessments of attractions, hotels,
restaurants and so forth are based on the author's own experience
and contain subjective opinions that may not reflect the publisher's
opinion or a reader's experience. We have tried to ensure accuracy
in this guide, but things do change, so please let us know if you have
any comments or corrections.

A CIP catalogue record for this book is available from the
British Library.

© AA Media Limited 2002, 2005, 2008, 2009
Maps © AA Media Limited 2002, 2005, 2008, 2009
New edition 2009

Cover design and binding style by permission of AA Publishing
Colour separation by Keenes, Andover
Printed and bound in China by Leo Paper Products

Find out more about AA Publishing and the wide range of travel
publications and services the AA provides by visiting our website at
www.theAA.com/bookshop

A03805
Maps in this title produced from mapping © KOMPASS GmbH,
A-6063 Rum/Innsbruck

The Magazine

A great holiday is more than just lying on a beach or shopping till you drop — to really get the most from your trip you need to know what makes the place tick. The Magazine provides an entertaining overview of some of the social, cultural and natural elements that make up the unique character of this engaging island.

Paradise Island?

Think Gran Canaria and what springs to mind? Is it cheap-and-cheerful package tours with year-round sunshine, fine beaches and watersports, or lively entertainment and night-time revellers? Scratch beneath the surface of this holiday island and you will find a much more sophisticated image.

The island's reputation a a tourist hotspot has brought prosperity as well as its problems, such as over-development and pollution.

At the end of the 20th century, a serious debate began in Gran Canaria about the future of tourism on the island. The buzz words today are "rural" and "quality", as Gran Canaria seeks to attract a new kind of visitor, interested in culture and history as well as sun, sea and sand. Grants are available to fund rural tourism projects, from the renovation of cave houses to the restoration of the *caminos reales* (royal paths). The newest resorts offer conference centres, golf-courses, marinas and luxury hotels.

Left: Canary pines on Pinar de Tambada
Above: A hibiscus flower

GOOD ADVICE

"Rheumatism, neuralgia, gout, scrofula, venereal and other diseases find the climate most suitable...if strength permits, excursions should frequently be made to the hills or to the mountains, the change of air, even if only for a few hours, being of great advantage. All hotels will provide luncheon in a basket." A Samuel Brown, *Madeira, Canary Islands and Azores: A Practical and Complete Guide for the use of Tourists and Invalids* (1889)

ALTERNATIVE CLUBBING

Gran Canaria has the perfect climate for golf that enables the possibility to play 365 days a year. The first course on the island, Real Club de Golf de Las Palmas, was inaugurated in 1891, and was sampled by the early British tourists and resident ex-pats on the island. But it is in the first decade of the 21st century that a complete infrastructure has developed around golf on Gran Canaria, with golf resort luxury hotels rapidly becoming big business. There are currently nine first-rate golf courses, four in the vicinity of Las Palmas in the north and five around the resorts of the south, all set against a variety of stunning backdrops.

The challenge of the 21st century is to continue to attract tourists without upsetting the delicate balance of a fragile environment and a small island culture. Rural tourism initiatives have seen the growth of country hotels, restored with the discerning tourist in mind.

How it all began

Tourists had already been visiting Gran Canaria for more than a century, and early travellers, such as Briton A Samler Brown, had written about the health benefits of the island's year-round spring climate. Until the 1960s, however, the only tourist resort on Gran Canaria was Playa de las Canteras in Las Palmas (➤ 65, picture top right) and Maspalomas was little more than a desert. Nobody could have imagined that within a generation it would be a vast holiday complex welcoming some three million foreign visitors a year.

Since the Spanish Conquest in 1478, Gran Canaria has tended to rely on a single cash crop as its main source of income. Sugar, wine, cochineal (a natural dye

The course at Campo de Golf, Bandama

produced by insects feeding on the prickly pear plant) and bananas have all had their day, and the latest monoculture is tourism. The island is totally dependent on tourism – it provides almost 80 per cent of the gross domestic product – but people are asking what can make it sustainable.

The first "urbanisations" on Gran Canaria were pioneered by Alejandro del Castillo, Conde de la Vega Grande, who was quick to spot the potential of his vast country estates in the south. By 1974, when Gando Airport opened, Playa del Inglés (► 127–129) had been built on the Maspalomas sand dunes and Gran Canaria was receiving almost a million tourists a year. So it would seem that Gran Canaria became a victim of its own success. To sustain the growing numbers of visitors but at the same time protect the environment and lose its reputation as a raucous package tour destination, it is pulling out all the stops to promote a new image – and it looks like it might just succeed.

VENEGUERA

The arguments that raged throughout the 1990s over the remote beach of Veneguera (► 141) symbolised the ongoing battle between get-rich-quick developers and ecologists determined to preserve the last unspoiled corners of the island. Although Veneguera was eventually sold for development, it remains the westernmost limit of tourism on the south coast.

Modern cave houses in the Barranco de Guayadeque

Shaping the course
OF HISTORY

Because of its strategic position between Europe, Africa and America, Gran Canaria has found itself at the centre of major events involving some of the key characters in European history.

Christopher Columbus (1451–1506)

Columbus, or Cristobal Colón to the Spaniards, was born in Italy, but it was the Spanish monarchs Ferdinand and Isabella who sponsored his attempt to discover a western sea route to India in 1492.

Setting out from Spain in the caravel *Santa María*, he called in at the Canary Islands, at that time the last port of call in the known world. His log book speaks of putting in at Las Palmas for repairs, though some historians maintain that although he sent his boat to Las Palmas he preferred to stay on La Gomera, where he was having an affair with the Countess Beatriz de Bobadilla. On his first voyage to the New World, Columbus discovered Cuba and

Above: Christopher Columbus
Top: Interview with Queen Isabel

Hispaniola (Haiti) and returned in triumph to the Spanish court. It is likely that he also called in at Las Palmas and stayed at what is now the Casa de Colón (▶ 59–60) during his third and fourth voyages to America, which took place between 1498 and 1504.

Sir Francis Drake (c1540–96)

One person who conspicuously failed to conquer was Sir Francis Drake, who launched an unsuccessful attack on Las Palmas in 1595. After his victory over the Spanish Armada in 1588, he continued his expeditions against the Spanish, which had earlier brought him great wealth from his capture of tobacco, sugar, spices and slaves. Driven back from Las Palmas, he sailed to the Caribbean, where he died of dysentery and was buried at sea. His defeat at Las Palmas is commemorated every year on 6 October with a festival on the peninsula of La Isleta.

Sir Francis Drake's defeat at Las Palmas is commemorated annually

Francisco Franco (1892–1975)

The military revolt that ushered in the Spanish Civil War (1936–39) and the long period of dictatorship that followed had its roots in the Canary Islands. The Popular Front government elected in Madrid in 1936 had feared an uprising from right-wing generals and had dispatched them to far-flung outposts of Spain. Among them was General Franco, who

was posted to Tenerife. He and his fellow conspirators hatched a plot to overthrow the régime, and the commander of the Las Palmas garrison was shot dead in suspicious circumstances. Franco came for the funeral, and a British plane, which had been chartered from Croydon, ostensibly by holidaymakers, flew him out of Gando, the only airfield in the Canaries, to take charge of the élite Spanish African army in Melilla, a Spanish enclave on the north coast of Morocco. Franco spent his final night in Las Palmas at the Hotel Madrid and announced his rebellion from the military headquarters in Parque San Telmo (▶ 62).

The *Illustrated London News* carried this picture of Franco in 1936

Cavemen of the Canaries

"They kept lard and fat in earthenware jars, and fragrant woods for the needs of the dead; anointing them, smoking them and putting them into burnt sand... after 15 or 20 days, they placed them in the caves, if they were of the nobility; the rest they put in wasteland or lava rocks, making a hollow among the rocks and then covering them with mounds of stones."

First impressions

What did the Spanish conquerors find when they arrived on Gran Canaria in the 15th century? The words of Gómez Escudero (below left) give an example. They found a people who had never seen a wheel, had no knowledge of metals, and despite the fact that their ancestors had probably arrived from Africa by boat, did not appear to know how to sail. A people who lived in harmony with nature, totally untouched by the wars, the scientific discoveries and the artistic movements of medieval Europe. A people who made their homes in Stone Age villages of cave houses, yet with a degree of technical knowledge and social organisation that many societies of today would envy.

Guanche lifestyle

So what was life like for these aboriginal cavemen, who have come to be known as the Guanches? From the accounts of the early invaders, we know that they were exceptionally tall and fair-haired, traits which can still be seen in many Canarios today. They lived either in natural caves or in

Left: Roque Bentaiga
Above: Statue at Parque Dormas

artificial cave dwellings which they carved out of the rock using primitive tools of stone or bone. They grew barley and wheat, which they toasted and ground to make *gofio* (a type of flour) and also ate wild berries and figs. Goats, sheep and pigs were reared for milk, meat and hide, and fish and shellfish were gathered using nets. They wove baskets out of palm leaves, made simple red ochre pottery, and carved wood into plates, mugs, jewellery, weapons, doors and coffins. Wrestling (► 34) and stick-fighting contests were organised, both for duels and as entertainment. When people were wounded in battle they treated their injuries by trepanation (a surgical operation to the skull) or drew blood using a flintstone and made purgatives out of thistles.

Guanche Society

Guanche society was strictly feudal in nature, with clear social divisions between the nobles and the peasantry, who were easily distinguished by their shaven heads. Gran Canaria was divided into two kingdoms, based at Telde (► 92) and Gáldar (► 95), each ruled by a *guanarteme* (king). Next down from the king, the most powerful figure was the *faycán* (viceroy), who acted as judge and high priest. The nobles would meet under a dragon tree or in a tagoror (assembly house) to take decisions affecting the community. Grain was stored in communal granaries such as Cenobio de Valerón (➤ 86–87), and tithes were imposed on every citizen so that surplus grain could be reserved for periods of drought. The system of justice included execution by hanging or by dropping a large boulder onto the head, with lesser crimes punishable by the principle of "an eye for an eye". Although they had no contact with any other society, many of the ideas developed by the Guanches were in the mainstream of European democratic thought.

Guanche religion

Religion centred on Alcorán, the Supreme Creator, who was identified with sun, rain, mountains and the fertility of the earth. The Guanches also worshipped idols, many representing the female figure, such as those which can be seen at the Museo Canario in Las Palmas (➤ 52–55).

> Guanche society was feudal in nature with clear social divisions

Religious ceremonies were sometimes carried out by the *harimaguadas* (vestal virgins), nuns who were confined to a convent for life. Other young women would be sent to the convent and fed a rich diet in preparation for marriage and childbirth, for which wide hips were considered essential.

The most remarkable feature of Guanche spirituality was their practice of mummifying their dead, which has led to speculation that the Guanches

Actors show how poles were used as weapons and for vaulting at Mundo Aborigen

were descended from the ancient Egyptians. As in many societies, the
men who carried out this practice were treated as outsiders and excluded
from the life of the community.

Cave-dwelling today

Some of the cave houses in Gran Canaria have continued to be occupied
right up to the present day by people seeking an alternative lifestyle or
by villagers who appreciate the fact that they are cooler in summer and
warmer in winter than conventional homes. The cavemen who originally
inhabited them probably wouldn't recognise them today, however, with
their additional telephones and satellite dishes. The best places for seeing
cave houses are Artenara (➤ 32–33) and La Atalaya (➤ 79), the suburbs
of Telde (➤ 92) and the Barranco de Guayadeque (➤ 124–126)

Aboriginal world

For more insight into the lives of the Guanches, visit the Museo Canario in
Las Palmas (➤ 52–55) or Mundo Aborigen (➤ 138).

The death of the Guanches

When Juan Rejón landed at Las Palmas in 1478, Gran Canaria was ruled
by two Guanche kings. The *guanarteme* of Telde, Doramas, resisted the
Spanish invasion and was killed at Arucas in 1481. Tenesor Samidan,
king of Gáldar, was captured, converted to Christianity and taken to Spain.
He returned to Gran Canaria in 1483 as Don Fernando Guanarteme in
an effort to persuade his people to surrender before the Spaniards' final
assault. Many did so, but others retreated to their stronghold at Fortaleza
Grande and threw themselves off the cliffs rather than submit. Within a
few years the Guanches had effectively been wiped out – though there
are those who maintain that they never disappeared and that the present
Canario population is largely descended from the Guanches.

Openings in the rockface at Cuatro Puertas

TOP Island hits for...

There are many reasons for visiting Gran Canaria, with attractions for families, couples and singles. Below are just a few suggestions.

Watching the Sunset...
Cruz de Tejeda, from the hill behind El Refugio Hotel (➤ 117)
The terrace of the Riu Maspalomas hotel in Playa del Inglés (➤ 144)
Pinar de Tamadaba (pine forest; ➤ 106)
The harbour at Puerto de la Aldea (➤ 142)
The cliff path from Puerto Rico to Playa de los Amadores (➤ 141)

Getting a View
Artenara (➤ 106) – the view of the central sierra (picture top left) from the Rio de Janeiro-style statue of Christ
Mirador del Balcón (➤ 90) – the view over the wild west coast
The view across the dunes from the *mirador* behind Riu Palace Maspalomas Hotel (➤ 144)
Puerto de las Nieves (➤ 90) – the view over the harbour from the San Nicolás de Tolentino road

Being Out on the Town...
Casino Las Palmas, Hotel Santa Catalina, Las Palmas (➤ 66, 72)
Pacha, Calle Simón Bolivár, Las Palmas
Metro Centre, Playa del Inglés (➤ 148)
Yumbo Centre, Playa del Inglés (➤ 148)

Sampling a taste of Gran Canaria...
Casa Montesdeoca, Las Palmas (➤ 71)
El Padrino, Las Palmas (➤ 68)

La Esquina, Artenara (► 117)
La Casa Vieja, Playa del Inglés (► 145)
Tagoror, Barranco de Guayadeque (► 145)
La Bodeguilla Juananá, Puerto de Mogán
(► 146)

Living in Luxury
Rui Grand Palace, Maspalomas (► 144)
H10 Playa Meloneras, Las Meloneras (► 143)
Hotel Cordial Mogán Playa, Puerto de Mogán
(► 144)

Staying in the Hills
El Refugio (► 117)

Getting the Family Out and About
Palmitos Parque (► 134–135)
Cocodrilo (► 141)
Sioux City (► 141)
Camel trekking (► 149)

Popular Beaches
Maspalomas (► 130; picture middle left and
right), stunning undulating sand
Las Canteras (► 65) – the beach comes right up
to the city
Puerto Rico (► 139) – perfect for families
Sardina (► 96) – to get away from it all

Bringing home a piece of Gran Canaria
Mojo sauce – to spice up any meal
Bone-handled knives – wonderful intricate
craftwork (pictured right)
Canarian wooden balconies – a pretty replica
from a traditional Canarian home
Aloe vera products – smother yourself in this
healthy skin care option

Practising your swing
Real Club de Golf de Las Palmas (► 80, 97),
Caldera de Bandama – the oldest golf club on
the island
Anfi Tauro Golf (► 150), Tauro – spectacular
landscape of palm trees and lakes, backed by
volcanic mountains
Lopesan Meloneras Golf, Meloneras (► 159) –
the latest course to hit the scene

Getting back to
Nature

Rural tourism highlights the exceptional scenery and endemic flora and fauna in the natural reserves, an ideal terrain for superb hiking. Hotels and guesthouses are opening up away from the south-coast resorts advocating walking, cycling and horse riding.

Although it measures barely 50km (31 miles) across at its widest point, Gran Canaria has often been described as a continent in miniature. Within this small island you find tall mountains, deep valleys, pine and laurel forests, rocky cliffs, sand dunes, barren hillsides and tropical valleys bursting with ripe fruit. The island is almost circular in shape and resembles a volcanic cone, with a summit at the centre and a succession of *barrancos* (gorges) radiating out towards the sea like the spokes of a giant bicycle wheel. The northeasterly trade winds that blow in from the coast bring misty clouds which stack up against the central sierra, dividing the island into the humid north and the parched, sunny south.

Biodiversity
In 2005, Gran Canaria was designated a World Biosphere Reserve, which covers almost half the geographical space of the island and includes six rural towns with some 18,000 inhabitants, most of whom are involved in traditional activities. The island's geographic isolation has meant that of the 600 recognised species of vascular plants within the reserve, 95 are endemic to the island and a further 101 to the Canary Islands.

Walk the walk
The island offers wonderful hiking possibilities to both the casual walker and the experienced hiker. There is an extensive network of trails throughout the 32 protected natural areas, where you can climb mountains, trek through the *barrancos*, meander through forests or head for the dunes. In fact, the entire dramatic and rugged west coast has been declared a national park. For those preferring two wheels, cycling is popular and mountain bikes are available to rent.

The dam of La Sorrueda near Santa Lucia de Tirajana is surrounded by palm groves

A bird-of-paradise flower (strelitzia); the species is abundant on the island

National parks and nature reserves

If you don't want to get your boots dirty, you can always drive to one of the beautiful parks and reserves on the island, many of which have designated picnic areas. A trip to the Parque National at Tambada, with its delightful pine forest and stunning views, is rewarding. Other parks of interest include Pilancones, the Nublo with its dramatic peak (► 110) and the dunes at Maspalomas, a protected nature reserve.

> The island offers wonderful hiking possibilities

Plantlife

With its abundance of microclimates, the island supports a large variety of endemic plants, many of which can be seen at the Jardín Canario near Las Palmas (► 81–82). Imported species such as bougainvillea, hibiscus, poinsettia and strelitzia (bird-of-paradise) thrive in parks and gardens.

The Canary

Visitors are often disappointed to find that the native canary (*serenus canaria*) is actually muddy brown in colour and much quieter than the domesticated songbird, whose yellow plumage and distinctive voice are the result of more than 400 years of breeding. Contrary to popular belief, the canary almost certainly takes its name from the islands rather than the other way round – the Canary Islands probably were named after the large dogs (*canes* in Latin) which the Romans found there when they arrived.

CANARIAN FLORA

There are nearly 2,000 different species of plants in the Canary Islands, of which around 700 are endemic (exclusive to the islands). Many are only of interest to botanists, but the species mentioned below are all quite remarkable and can usually be easily seen.

■ **Canary pine (*pinus canariensis*):** this tall pine tree is found in the Central Mountains growing to a height of 60m (197 feet). Its resinous bark has the ability to survive forest fires, so it can live for hundreds of years. The wood of the Canary pine, known as tea, is used in the construction of ceilings and balconies.

■ **Candelabra spurge (*euphorbia canariensis*):** this cactus-like shrub (below) is found on rocky hillsides. It has a red fruit and a white milky sap which is used in traditional herbal remedies. It is distinguished by its spindly arms which can grow to heights of 2m (6 feet).

■ **Dragon tree (*dracaena draco*):** this distinctive tree, with its thick trunk and spiky green crown, is one of the last survivors of the Ice Age. Its blood-red resin was used as a medicine by the Guanches, who named it 'dragon's blood' and ascribed it magical powers. There are some fine examples of dragon trees in the Jardín Canario (▶ 81–82).

■ **White tajinaste (*echium decaisnei*):** a native variety of borage found in dry, rocky areas near the south coast. It has sword-shaped leaves and tiny white flowers which bloom in spring. A related plant, the blue tajinaste, grows wild in the Central Mountains.

■ **Aloe vera (family *Asphodelaceae*):** this spiky plant grows abundantly throughout the island and is the mainstay of an industry devoted to the production of beauty and health products. Complete shops are near-temples to the plant, such as Miguel Crespo in Las Palmas, with a plethora of soaps, creams and lotions to indulge the skin.

A taste of the CANARIES

Is there such a thing as authentic Canarian cuisine? Away from the standard international choices on offer in the main tourist resorts, a different type of cooking survives in the fishing ports and inland towns and villages of Gran Canaria.

This is traditional Spanish country cooking, introduced by immigrants and adapted to local ingredients with a few Caribbean influences thrown in. Herbs and spices are widely used, including garlic, cumin, coriander, saffron, oregano and thyme, while other essential ingredients are olive oil, potatoes and tomatoes. Bananas, mango, papaya and avocado often appear in salads and desserts and as unusual accompaniments to meat and fish.

Mojo
The standard accompaniment to all Canarian cuisine is *mojo* sauce. This can be bought in jars but most chefs make their own. There are two basic types: *mojo picón* (spicy red *mojo*) and *mojo verde* (green *mojo*). *Mojo picón* is a blend of chilli peppers, garlic, cumin, paprika and vinegar, served cold with grilled meat, *gofio*, bread and potatoes. For *mojo verde*, fresh coriander leaves replace the chilli, making it an ideal accompaniment for fish.

Bienmesabe
This popular dessert is made by adding ground almonds and egg yolks to a sugar syrup. Its name means "it tastes good to me" *Bienmesabe* has the consistency of honey and is often served with baked bananas or poured over ice-cream.

Cheese
Q*ueso* (cheese, picture right)) is generally eaten as a starter. Try are *queso tierno* (a soft goat's cheese), *queso curado* (mature sheep's or goat's cheese, such as Majorero from Fuerteventura) and *queso de flor*, produced in the highlands of Guía and curdled with thistle flowers.

Fish

Among the Atlantic fish caught in the waters off Gran Canaria are *cherne*, the most common, (a kind of grouper), *sama* (bream) and *vieja* (parrotfish). In fishing ports such as Arguineguín and Puerto de Mogán, there's always *pescado fresco* (fresh fish) on the menu.

Gofio

Gofio, a flour made by grinding toasted barley, maize (corn) or wheat, is the traditional Canarian comfort food. This was the staple diet of the Guanches and it has survived almost unchanged to this day. Canarians stir it into warm milk as a breakfast porridge or as a drink for young babies; it is rolled into dumplings and added to soups and stews. It can be kneaded with bananas, blended with wine and egg yolk, or eaten plain with fresh cheese and *mojo* sauce. It can even be made into ice-cream. Everybody should try it once, but most people seem to agree that once is enough.

CANARIAN SPECIALITIES

- **Conejo en salmorejo** – rabbit marinated in garlic, parsley, oregano, thyme and vinegar, then basted in wine and served in an earthenware dish with *papas*
- **Arrugadas gofio escaldado** – *gofio* stirred into fish stock to produce a thick paste
- **Papas arrugadas** – literally "wrinkled" potatoes, boiled in their skins in salty water and eaten with red mojo sauce (below right)
- **Potaje de berros** – watercress soup, which may also include potatoes, sweet potatoes and bacon
- **Puchero canario** – a hearty meat and vegetable casserole which typically contains beef, pork, chicken, sausage, chickpeas, marrow, sweetcorn, carrots, beans, tomato, onion and pears, served with *gofio* dumplings to soak up the stock
- **Rancho canario** – a stew of meat, potatoes, chickpeas, tomatoes and noodles
- **Ropa vieja** – literally "old clothes", this consists of chickpeas fried with diced meat and vegetables and was invented as a way of using up leftovers
- **Sancocho** – the most typical Canarian dish of all, this is salt fish and potato stew served with *papas arrugadas*, *gofio* and *mojo* sauce

Keep it in the
family

Bearing in mind not many kids – no matter what age – do scenery, most activities that interest them are going to be around the busy beachside resorts, where you will find waterparks, theme parks, karting, camel-riding, watersports, and much more.

Taking that into consideration, Gran Canaria can offer the perfect holiday for families with its gentle climate and safe beaches. There is a whole host of accommodation suitable for those with children, although self-catering villas or apartments are a popular choice. Many of the larger hotel complexes, however, have holiday clubs to entertain the youngsters.

On Dry Land
For something totally different, encourage the family to get up close and personal to a camel, by taking a ride across the sand dunes in the style of Lawrence of Arabia. A more conventional experience in the saddle is on horseback into the hills. Most children love animals, and a visit to Palmitos Parque (► 134–135), with its parrot shows, or Cocodrillo Park, where you can get close to a tiger, monkey or a crocodile, is certain to fulfil their passion.

Water Babies

Thrill-seeking teenagers can take their pick from a host of watersports ranging from windsurfing and body boarding to scuba diving and snorkelling. Beach Leisure (tel 928/772-872; www.beachleisure.net) near San Agustín gives older kids the chance to kitesurf, kayak or waterski. For younger children there are pedaloes and banana rides and for the toddlers there's nothing better than splashing in the surf and making sand castles. All the family can enjoy a boat excursion either on board a glass-bottomed boat, a catamaran, or a real submarine, which descends 20m (66 feet) under the surface. A special treat that all children love is a dolphin spotting exploration, but sadly they can often come back disappointed.

Palmitos Parque (far left) and Sioux City (left) are popular with children

No Time Too Get Bored

If the family have exhausted all ideas and are still looking for more here are few suggestions: swim with sea lions, hire a mountain bike, visit a butterfly farm, encounter cowboys and Indians in Sioux City (➤ 141), join in at a local festival, play golf–and if the kids are still going strong do it all again.

Children can enjoy snorkelling and karting alongside adults

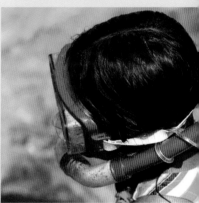

Thrills and Adventures

Children's adrenalin (and the adults, too) will be tested by the roller coasters at Holiday World (➤ 141). The Adventure Park at Bahía Feliz will give any budding racing driver a thrill with its quad bikes and mountain buggy rides, while the Go Karting Club will further develop their driving skills. When you all feel the need to cool off Aqualand (➤ 141) or Atlantica Fun Park offers exciting water slides and rubber ring rides with a big splashes.

Taking it to the
EXTREME

The craze for extreme sports and activities, as in so many other parts of the world, have hit the Canary Islands and even the most hardened adrenalin junkie will find something to thrill here on Gran Canaria.

Take to the Waves

Experienced windsurfers (top right) and sailors will find plenty of opportunities to push their skills to the limit. The toughest conditions for windsurfing can be found in the north and special high-wind excursions to this area are arranged by Club Mistral (tel: 928/157-158), based at Playa Tarjalillo, Bahía Feliz. Serious windsurfers like to ride the massive waves at Pozo Izquierdo, home to The Centro Internacional de Windsurf (tel: 928/121-400). The experts demonstrate how it's done when the World Windsurfing Pro Tour Championships take place in July in different locations throughout the island—the Grand Slam features competitions in race, wave and freestyle classes. The Canary Islands have been dubbed the "Hawaii of Europe", because of their perfect surfing conditions, and the fastest growing sport on the waves is kitesurfing. Okite (tel: 928/772-872; www.beachleisure.net, is located on Las Barras beach near San Agustín.

Flying High

Take to the skies with Skydive Gran Canaria (www.skydivegrancanaria.es) and then experience a freefall tandem jump to bring you down to earth. This awesome sensation, which takes place over the dunes, lasts about 55 seconds with the parachute opening at around 1,500m (4,920 feet). You take off from the Real Aeroclub Gran Canaria at El Berriel on the southeast coast, and the round-trip over the island lasts around 20 minutes. For those seeking a little less drama in the sky, parascending is available at Puerto Rico and Playa del Inglés.

Although perhaps a bit sedate for extreme sport enthusiasts, sightseeing flights give you a bird's-eye view of the island (www.canaryislandflights.net). There is room for three passengers on the Piper Cherokee 28 and there is an English commentary. Alternatively, take a tour by helicopter with Islas Helicopters (www.islashelicopters.com). Three different tours are offered – the Tour Roque Nublo (20 minutes); the Tour Costa Sur (10 minutes); and the Tour Isla Grande (30 minutes). Flights take off from the Real Aeroclub.

> The fastest growing sport on the waves is kitesurfing

Overland Adventure

Travel deep into the mountains on a buggy or quad safari with Canarias eXtreme Sports and Adventure (www.canariasextreme.com). On the mountain tour you go off road and up to a height of 1,200m (3,936 feet) across terrain particularly suited to buggies or quads. Alternatively, hire a mountain bike (above) and pedal up into the hills.

Top left: A climber training in Ayacata

DELVING DEEP
into the

The deep blue seas off the coast of Gran Canaria, reputed to be one of the prime dive sites in Europe, entice you to explore a mysterious underwater world and make the acquaintance of all who lurk there. There are various ways of taking part in such an experience and, if you're lucky, you might witness anything from angel sharks, butterfly rays and seahorses to dolphins, parrotfish and even the occasional turtle or octopus.

Take a Dive

One of the best dive sites on the island is at El Cabrón Marine Reserve, just outside Arinaga, and those who venture down will be entranced by the fascinating, colourful and varied species of marine life here. There's exceptional underwater scenery, too, with shipwrecks, caves and massive vertical drops. Even if you have never dived before you will still see a great deal in your first 40 minutes in the water. The water temperature is ideal at around 20°C, with a visibility of between 15m and 30m (49 feet and 98 feet). Around the island there are other excellent dive sites including Las Palmas, Pozo Izquierdo, Arguineguín, Puerto Rico and Puerto de Mogán, and first-class tuition is normally offered by most establishments, suitable for the novice as well as the experienced diver. If you are not ready for the full-on dive there are also superb opportunities for snorkelling in all of these locations.

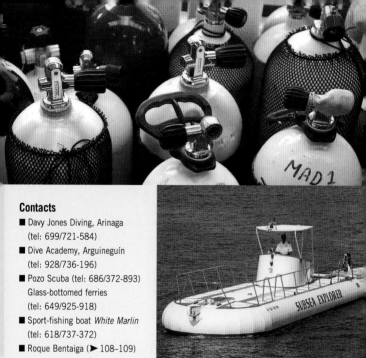

Contacts
- ■ Davy Jones Diving, Arinaga
  (tel: 699/721-584)
- ■ Dive Academy, Arguineguín
  (tel: 928/736-196)
- ■ Pozo Scuba (tel: 686/372-893)
  Glass-bottomed ferries
  (tel: 649/925-918)
- ■ Sport-fishing boat *White Marlin*
  (tel: 618/737-372)
- ■ Roque Bentaiga (► 108–109)

Top left: Deep-sea fisherman   **Scuba tanks (top) in a diving shop**

Boat Trips

For those who prefer to peer into the depths from the comfort of a boat, an excursion on the Yellow Submarine, which is based in Puerto de Mogán (► 136–137), will open your eyes to what lies beneath the surface. Also, glass-bottomed boats and catamarans ply the waters, often providing a ferry service from one resort to another, and offer a completely different perspective on things. There is also a chance to spot dolphins, or even whales, on a boat trip from Puerto Rico (*Explorer* pictured above).

Sea Fishing

If you want to try your hand at sea fishing and catch one of those creatures under the water, Puerto Rico is one of the world capitals of big game fishing. More than 30 world records have been set here. Among the fish which swim in the waters off the south coast of Gran Canaria are albacora, big-eye, yellowfin and skipjack tuna, bonito, barracuda, swordfish, shark and wahoo, but the ultimate prize is the blue marlin, which can weigh anything between 250 and 500kg (550–1,100lbs). To see a blue marlin being caught is to witness an epic sporting battle between man and beast and you are never quite sure who is going to win. If you don't want to fish, most boats will also accept paying spectators at a slightly lower price. Apart from the excitement of watching the fishers at work, there is a good chance of spotting basking dolphins and possibly flying fish.

FIESTA!

Nowhere in Spain is the traditional pre-Lenten Carnival celebrated with as much gusto as it is in the Canary Islands. Each year Gran Canaria and Tenerife compete to stage the biggest parades this side of Rio de Janerio.

For nearly three weeks in February, Las Palmas is one giant party, with acrobats, clowns, magicians, brass bands, salsa music, fireworks and riotous fancy-dress parades.

The dates vary from year to year, but it all starts around nine weeks before Easter with the Verbena de la Sábana (Sheet Party), where the participants are dressed in a sheet and little else. Like most of the Carnival events, this takes place on an open-air stage in Parque Santa Catalina (➤ 63–64). It is followed by the election of the Carnival Queen and the Children's Queen and a week of street parties, singing contests and body-painting competitions leading up to the final weekend.

> The Burial of the Sardine symbolises the end of Carnival

The wildest night of all is the Friday before Shrove Tuesday, when the Carnival Drag Queen is chosen. The grand parade takes place the following day, with the Carnival Queen on the leading float in a glittering

outfit of sequins, spangles and feathers. The parade starts in La Isleta and continues for several hours, ending at midnight with an open-air *mogollón* (fancy-dress party). Most of Las Palmas joins in, wearing outrageous masks and costumes.

Sunday is the day of the children's Carnival, while Monday sees the start of the *velatorio* (death watch), when a huge papier-mâché sardine is carried in mock funeral procession through the streets by a group of mourners dressed in black drag. The Burial of the Sardine, which symbolises the end of Carnival and the beginning of Lent, takes place on Shrove Tuesday on Playa de las Canteras (➤ 65), to the accompaniment of bonfires and fireworks. Carnival may have ended in Las Palmas but it continues further south, with a weekend of processions and parties around the Yumbo Centre in Playa del Inglés (➤ 148).

Top; **Baja de Rama festival in Agaete**

Right: **Carnival queen in Las Palmas**

The Virgin of the Cave

The last Sunday in August witnesses the climax of the fiesta of the Virgin of the Cave in Artenara (➤ 106). At the beginning of the fiesta, the carved wooden statue of the Virgin is taken out of her cave chapel and placed in the parish church, where the villagers come all week to pay their respects The priest gives his blessing, the worshippers file out and the Virgin is carried around the town by four hefty men, accompanied by a brass band, a military guard of honour, an occasional burst of fireworks and a procession of civic dignitaries in suits.

> ## The Virgin is carried around the town by four hefty men

A folklore performance entertains the crowds. Folk groups from Gran Canaria and Tenerife sing and dance, dressed in extravagantly embroidered waistcoats and skirts. As dusk falls, people climb to the *mirador* above the village to watch the sun set over Tenerife.

At 9pm the concert ends and the final procession begins. A burst of fireworks lights up the sky and flaming torches spring into life as the mayor lights the touch-paper. The Virgin is carried slowly back to her

Top: La Ermita de la Cuevita church, Artenara; detail of the Virgin statue (top right)

cave, with more music and fireworks followed by a solemn climb. The procession reaches the chapel, the fireworks go off once again, a spectacular display which lasts for 20 minutes. The Virgin is placed back in her chapel, the priest says his final blessings and the villagers return to the square to salsa the night away

La Rama

One of the chroniclers of the conquest recalled how the Guanche priests "gathered the people together and led them to the sea-shore, with boughs and branches in their hands, calling out loud as they beat the water with their boughs." This tradition continues today at the fiestas of Bajada de la Rama in Agaete (► 100) and San Nicolás de Tolentino (► 142).

Traditional dancer in Las Palmas

LUCHA CANARIA

Two men enter the arena barefoot. They grip each other tightly. Welcome to *lucha canaria* (Canarian wrestling; left), the oldest sport in the Canary Islands.

The sport has its origins in the fights that used to take place between rival Guanche kingdoms and tribes. Chronicles of the Conquest describe a wrestling match between fighters from Telde and Gáldar in order to resolve a dispute over grazing rights. You can see displays at all the main festivals, and the regular bouts in the local island leagues attract an attendance that is second only to football.

It may look like little more than a brawl, but this is a sport with detailed rules and a strict code of conduct. No part of a wrestler's body other than the soles of his feet may touch the ground and the aim is to force his opponent onto the sand. There are 12 players in each team which takes part in a series of best-of-three *bregas* (bouts). Although strength is important, dexterity and finesse are equally useful. The contest always ends as it began – with a handshake.

Where to See it

Find out where a Canarian wrestling match is taking place by looking in *La Provincia*, whose Wednesday edition lists all the upcoming weekend fixtures. In the south coast resorts, the teams to follow are Arguineguín and Maspalomas, who wrestle in the suburb of El Tablero.

Stick-fighting

Juego del palo (stick-fighting) is another traditional Canarian sport with its origins in the ancient art of duelling. Two men face one another with *garrotes* (2m/6ft long wooden staffs). The idea is to strike your opponent with the stick while at the same time dodging the blows. You can sometimes see demonstrations at local fiestas in Gran Canaria.

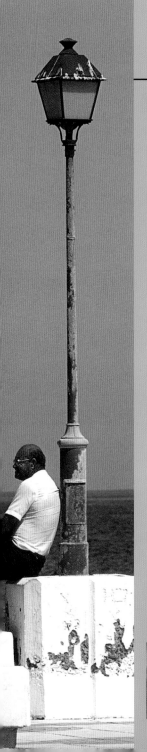

Finding Your Feet

First Two Hours

Arriving at Gando Airport

The main point of entry is the **Aeropuerto de Gando**, 22km (14 miles) south of Las Palmas on the east coast of the island.

- Most travellers on package holidays are met at the airport by representatives of the **tour operator** and transported to their accommodation by bus.
- The major **car hire** companies have desks in the arrivals hall, and there are also currency exchange facilities.

Getting to Las Palmas from Gando Airport

- The quickest but most expensive option is to take a **taxi** from outside the airport building.
- There is also a frequent, reliable and inexpensive **bus** service to Las Palmas (www.globalsu.net). Bus No 60 leaves from outside the airport terminal every 45 minutes from 6am to 7pm and then hourly until 1am. The journey takes around 30 minutes. The buses arrive at the central bus station beside Parque San Telmo, where there are connections to local buses and taxis as well as buses to the rest of the island.

Getting to the South Coast from Gando Airport

- The quickest but most expensive option is to take a **taxi** from outside the airport building. Costs vary.
- The other alternative is to get there by **bus**. Bus No 66 leaves for Playa del Inglés and Maspalomas every hour from 7am to 10pm. The journey takes around one hour. From Playa del Inglés there are regular connections to other south coast resorts, including Puerto Rico and Puerto de Mogán.

Arriving by Sea

- **Passenger and car ferries** from the Spanish mainland and the other Canary Islands arrive at Puerto de la Luz in Las Palmas.
- There is also a **fast ferry link** from Tenerife to Puerto de las Nieves, with a free shuttle bus to Las Palmas. The journey from Puerto de las Nieves to Las Palmas takes around 40 minutes by car.

Car Hire

- The major car hire companies have offices at the **airport**.
- You will generally save both time and money by **booking in advance**.
- To hire a car you must be **over 21**, and you will need a credit card, passport and driving licence.
- Car hire is **widely available** in Las Palmas and all the main resorts, so unless you are staying somewhere remote, it may be better to travel to your accommodation by bus and hire a car when you get there.
- **4WD** cars are available in all the main resorts but you need to book them in advance at the airport.
- If you are driving from the airport, the **GC1 motorway** leads north to Las Palmas and south to Puerto Rico.
- **Avis**: tel: 928/579-578; www.avis-europe.com
- **Europcar**: tel: 928/574-244; www.europcar.com
- **Hertz**: tel: 928/579-577; www.hertz.com

Security

Although Gran Canaria is no more dangerous than other popular tourist areas of Spain, it is important to remember that you are at your most vulnerable to theft when you first arrive in an unfamiliar destination.

■ It is advisable to keep your passport, money and other valuables in an inside pocket or money-belt and to lock them in a **safety deposit box** as soon as you arrive at your hotel or apartment.

■ Keep your **hand luggage**, including items such as cameras, with you at all times.

■ Do not leave any bags **unattended** while standing at a car hire desk or loading suitcases onto a bus.

■ **Petty crime** is particularly prevalent in the Santa Catalina and port districts of Las Palmas.

Tourist Information Offices

Most tourist office staff speak excellent English, and can issue maps and information in English.

Las Palmas

■ The **Patronato de Turismo** (Tourist Board) has its offices at Calle León y Castillo 17, a short walk from the bus station. Open: Mon–Fri 9–2, tel: 928/219-600; www.grancanaria.com.

■ There are also **tourist information offices** and kiosks in Parque San Telmo, Plaza de Hurtado Mendoza and Avenida Mesa y López as well as at the Pueblo Canario, on the promenade behind Playa las Canteras and at the Parque Santa Catalina, beside the terminal for the Guagua Turistica tour buses.

■ The information office at the **bus station** has maps and timetables, and sells discount tickets such as the *Bono-Guagua* and *Tarjeta Insular* (► 38).

South Coast

■ **Yumbo Centre**, Playa del Inglés, tel: 928/771-550. Open: Jul–Sep Mon–Fri 9–2, 3–8, Sat 9–1; Oct–Jun Mon–Fri 9–9, Sat 9–1.

■ **San Agustín**, Centro Comercial, El Portón, Local 11, tel: 928/769-262; www.maaspalomas.com. Open: Mon–Fri 9–2.

■ **Puerto Rico** has an office on Avenida de Mogán, near the bus stop on the roundabout at the entrance to the resort, tel: 928/158-804. Open: Mon–Fri 9–2.

Getting Around

The island's comparatively small size can be an advantage. Both Las Palmas and Maspalomas are just 30 minutes from the airport, and it is quite possible to drive round the whole island in a day (► 164).

Buses

For journeys to and from Las Palmas and the south coast resorts, the most economic and efficient way of getting about is by bus.

■ The company **Global** (www.globalsu.net) operates a comprehensive network of routes, with regular departures during the day and some night services.

■ **Timetables and maps** are available from the bus station in Las Palmas and the tourist office in Playa del Inglés.

■ The *Tarjeta Insular* discount card is good value for anyone travelling around the island by bus. The card is available from the bus station in Las Palmas and at kiosks and shops where the Tarjeta Insular symbol is displayed. It gives around €20 worth of travel at a 30 per cent discount. To use the card, simply tell the driver where you are going and insert the card into the machine at the front of the bus so that the fare can be deducted from your remaining credit.

Some of the most **useful bus lines** are:
■ **01** Las Palmas–Playa del Inglés–Puerto Rico–Puerto de Mogán
■ **30** Las Palmas–Playa del Inglés–Maspalomas
■ **32** Playa del Inglés–Puerto Rico–Puerto de Mogán
■ **66** Airport (Aeropuerto) Playa del Inglés–Faro de Maspalomas

City Buses
Las Palmas has its own bus company, **Guaguas Municipales** (www.guaguas. com), which operates a network of routes throughout the city.
■ Fares are flat-rate, but the *Bono-Guagua* discount card, available from newsagents, tobacconists and bus terminals, gives ten journeys for the price of six. The *Tarjeta Insular* (see above) is also valid on city buses.
■ The three **main routes** connect the old town to the port district. The most useful is No 1, which operates 24 hours a day and follows a direct route from Teatro Pérez Galdós to Parque San Telmo, Pueblo Canario and Parque Santa Catalina. Bus Nos 2 and 3 depart from Alameda de Colón and also pass through Parque Santa Catalina.
■ A detailed **city bus map** and **timetable** is available from the information office at the bus station beside Parque San Telmo.
■ The *Guagua Turística* is an open-top tour bus which makes a two-hour circuit of the city, beginning and ending in Parque Santa Catalina. Tickets cost €8 and are valid for a day; you can hop on and off as often as you like. The bus leaves Parque Santa Catalina every 30 minutes from 9:30 to 12:30 and from 2:45 to 5:45. You can also pick up the bus outside the central bus station on Parque San Telmo.

Taxis
■ Taxis can be identified by a **green light** on the top which when illuminated indicates that they are available for hire.
■ For local journeys, fares are **metered** and charges are usually reasonable.
■ If travelling outside municipal boundaries, the meter does not apply and it is best to **fix a fare in advance**.
■ You can usually **hail a taxi** on the street, but at busy times it is better to find a taxi rank or to book in advance.

Useful telephone numbers include:
■ 928/461-818 (Las Palmas)
■ 928/766-767 (San Agustín/Maspalomas/Playa del Inglés)
■ 928/152-740 (Puerto de Mogán)

Driving
If you want to explore the interior of Gran Canaria away from the coastal resorts, you will probably need to hire a car (► 36).
■ Driving in the **mountains** can be a challenge, with twisting roads and narrow bends demanding intense concentration.
■ Make sure you allow **plenty of time** for your journey and do not expect to cover more than 40km (25 miles) per hour.

- The only **fast roads** on the island are the GC1 motorway from Las Palmas to Puerto Rico and the GC2 from Las Palmas to Agaete.
- Be aware, most petrol stations close on Sunday afternoons.

Car Hire

- The **major international** car hire companies have offices at Gando Airport (► 36), in Las Palmas and in all the main resorts.
- **Local companies** also offer competitive deals, so unless you need a car immediately it is worth shopping around when you reach your resort.
- To **hire a car** you will need your passport, driving licence and credit card. Keep these papers on you at all times, along with the car hire documents.
- Check your **insurance cover** carefully. If you plan to drive on mountain tracks or to some of the more remote beaches, you will not be covered unless you hire a jeep or off-road (4WD) vehicle.

Driving Essentials

- Drive on the **right-hand** side of the road.
- **Seat belts** are compulsory for the driver and all passengers.
- The legal **alcohol** limit is 50mg alcohol per 100ml blood.
- **Speed limits** are 120kph (75mph) on motorways, 90kph (56mph) on main roads, 50kph (32mph) in urban areas and 20kph (12mph) in residential areas, unless otherwise indicated.
- **Dipped headlights** are compulsory in tunnels.
- Use your **horn** when overtaking and when approaching blind bends.
- **Fuel** is much cheaper than on mainland Spain and the cost even in summer 2008 was exceptionally good. Many filling stations are open 24 hours. Most stations accept credit cards.
- **Parking** is prohibited on white or yellow lines. Blue lines indicate a restricted parking area where you must purchase a ticket from a pay-and-display machine.
- **Theft** from hire cars is widespread. Never leave any items on display inside the car, and lock all valuables out of sight in the boot.

Organised Excursions

- Package tour operators offer numerous **excursions**, from jeep safaris to bus tours, which can be booked through your holiday representative.
- The **advantage** is that you can get around the island without hiring a car; the **drawbacks** are that they are expensive and you have no control over the itinerary.
- **Beware** of local companies offering free excursions – these are invariably combined with a hard-sell timeshare (► 40) or product demonstration.

Admission Charges

The cost of admission for museums and places of interest featured in the guide is indicated by the following price categories.

Inexpensive under €5
Moderate €5–€10
Expensive over €10

Accommodation

Most people arrive in Gran Canaria on package holidays with pre-booked accommodation. The majority of hotels and apartments are booked up by tour operators, so independent travellers may experience difficulties in finding somewhere to stay. Local tourist offices keep lists of apartments and may be able to help, but on the whole it is far better to book in advance.

Hotels
All hotels are officially graded by the Canarian government from one to five stars, with most establishments rated as three-star or higher. In three-star hotels and above, all rooms will have a private bathroom. Hotels are more expensive during the peak season from November to April. There is a second peak in July and August, when many Spanish families are on holiday. The quietest months are May, June, September and October.

Apartments
Many people, especially families, prefer the freedom of a self-catering apartment or villa. Apartments are graded from one to three keys, and even the simplest will usually have a bedroom, bathroom, lounge, kitchenette and balcony. Bed linen, towels and maid service are included in the price; equipment such as kettles and toasters can sometimes be hired for an extra charge. Aparthotels are large apartment blocks with all the facilities of a hotel, such as a swimming-pool, restaurant and evening entertainment.

Casas rurales
Casas rurales are village houses, cave dwellings and farmsteads which have been converted into holiday cottages. If you don't mind hiring a car and being based away from the beach, these offer a more authentic experience of Gran Canaria. Most are decorated in traditional style, though many also have swimming-pools. Rural houses can be let through the following agencies:
- **Gran Canaria Rural** (tel: 928/462-547; www.grancanariarural.com)
- **Grantural** (tel: 902/157-281; www.grantural.com)
- **Santa Lucia Rural** (tel: 928/330-262;www.santaluciarural.com)

Timeshare
Salespeople in the main resorts will invite you to demonstrations of timeshare properties, sometimes described as "vacation ownership". This involves buying the right to an annual holiday in a particular villa or apartment in return for a one-off down payment and an annual service charge. Some of the timeshare properties, such as those at Anfi del Mar, are extremely well designed and maintained, but you should be aware that the combined cost of service charge, flights, insurance and loss of interest can make this an expensive way of paying for your holiday. You should also think carefully about whether you want to spend your holiday in the same place every year.

Accommodation Prices
The symbols refer to the average cost of a double room in high season, generally November to April. All prices exclude 4.5 per cent sales tax (IGIC).

| € under €70 | €€ €70–€130 | €€€ over €130 |

Food and Drink

Most restaurants in Gran Canaria offer Canarian cuisine (► 22), together
with steaks, seafood dishes and traditional Spanish favourites such as
paella. Fresh fish is available all around the coast, particularly in fishing
ports such as Puerto de las Nieves, Puerto de Mogán and Arguineguín.

What and Where to Eat

- In the mountainous interior, the most common type of restaurant is a
  parrilla, a country-style grill specialising in barbecued, grilled and roasted
  meat.
- Resorts such as Puerto Rico and Playa del Inglés have a **full range of
  restaurants**, offering English breakfasts, hamburgers, pizzas, apple strudel
  and other reminders of home to an international clientele.
- Bars in Las Palmas and other towns serve ***tapas***, small portions of Spanish
  and Canarian snacks which can often take the place of a meal. These
  originated in the old Spanish custom of placing a free *tapa* (lid) of food,
  such as a saucer of olives, over a drink. Popular *tapas* include *pata de
  cerdo* (cold roast pork) and *queso curado* (mature cheese).
- One snack which is available everywhere, even in tourist areas, is ***papas
  arrugadas*** (salty boiled potatoes with *mojo* sauce – ► 23).
- The best places to buy **picnic food** are at the Mercado de Vegueta in Las
  Palmas (► 61), the weekly market at Vega de San Mateo (► 93), and
  supermarkets in all the main resorts.

Eating Out – A Practical Guide

- The traditional **mealtimes** are 1–4pm for lunch and 8–11pm for dinner,
  though many restaurants are open throughout the day to cater for the
  varying demands of locals and tourists.
- Many restaurants offer a ***menu del día***, a fixed-price menu of three courses
  with water or wine included. This is always available at lunchtime and
  sometimes in the evening, and usually represents good value.
- By law, **service** has to be included in the price, though there may be a
  nominal cover charge for items such as bread and olives. If you are happy
  with the service, it is customary to leave a tip of between 5 and 10 per
  cent. In bars, the tradition is to leave some small change on the counter.
- **Booking** is rarely necessary except at the smartest restaurants, though it is
  usually worth booking a table for Saturday dinner or Sunday lunch.
- **Vegetarians** could have a hard time as even vegetable dishes may contain
  pieces of meat or fish. Most restaurants will serve you a large *ensalada
  mixta* (mixed salad) with *tortilla* (potato omelette) or *queso* (cheese).
- It is **quite acceptable** to order two starters and no main course, or a single
  starter for two people to share.
- **Children's menus** are available in some of the resort restaurants, but if not
  you can always ask for a smaller portion of an adult dish.

Guide to Drinking

Mineral water is produced in Firgas and Teror and is available across the
island. Ask for *agua sin gas* (still) or *agua con gas* (sparkling).

The variety of fruit grown on Gran Canaria means that fresh **fruit juice**
is always a good choice. The most common is zumo de naranja (orange
juice), though some bars offer freshly squeezed mango, papaya, banana,
pineapple and kiwi fruit.

Coffee is usually served after the meal as *café solo*, a small shot of strong,
black coffee like an espresso. Other varieties are *café cortado* (espresso

> **Best...**
> **...for fish:**
> Bar Cofradía de Pescadores, Arguineguín (➤ 146);
> El Padrino, Calle Jesús Nazareno 1, Las Colorades (➤ 68);
> Restaurante Cofradía, Puerto de Mogán (➤ 146)
> **...for meat:**
> El Novillo Precoz 9, Calle Portugal, Las Palmas (➤ 67)
> Hao, Calle Tomás Arroyo Cardosa, Santa Lucía (➤ 117);
> Las Cumbres Canarias, Avenida de Tirajana, Playa del Inglés (➤ 145);
> **...for tapas:**
> El Herreño, Calle Mendizábal 5, Las Palmas (➤ 67)

with a dash of hot milk), *café con leche* (with lots of hot milk) and *café con leche condensada* (with condensed milk).

- The most popular brand of **beer** is Tropical, which is produced in Gran Canaria and comes either in bottles or on draught. Most bars also stock a range of imported beers.
- Small quantities of **wine** are produced on Gran Canaria and the other Canary Islands. One unusual choice is *malvasia* (malmsey), a white wine from Lanzarote which can be sweet or dry. The best wines from the Spanish mainland come from the region of La Rioja.
- The local **spirit** is rum from Arucas, the base for a number of liqueurs, including *ron miel* (honey rum) and *guindilla* (cherry liqueur). Spanish brandy is also popular and is sometimes added to *sangría*, a red wine and fruit punch.
- It is the custom in many restaurants to bring you a **liqueur** with your bill.

Restaurant Prices

Expect to pay per person for a meal, excluding drinks and service
€ under €15   €€ €15–€30   €€€ over €30

Shopping

Despite Spain's membership of the European Union, the Canary Islands have retained their special status as a free trade zone, with minimal import duties and a low rate of value added tax (VAT) – 5 per cent.

Many everyday items are considerably cheaper here than elsewhere. Alcohol, tobacco, perfume, jewellery, clothing and electronic goods are all sold cheaply at duty-free shops in Las Palmas and the south coast resorts.

Unlike elsewhere in the European Union, there are strict limits to the amount of goods which can be exported for personal use. The allowances to other European Union countries are 60cc of perfume, 1 litre of spirits, 2 litres of wine and either 200 cigarettes or 50 cigars.

Shopping Areas

- The biggest **range** of shops and merchandise is found in Las Palmas, especially at the La Ballena and Las Arenas shopping malls and along Avenida Mesa y López, which has two branches of the leading Spanish department store El Corte Inglés.
- The **shopping centres** of Playa del Inglés are busy seven days a week, but the emphasis here is on price rather than quality.

- **Supermarkets** in all of the south coast resorts sell a wide range of local and imported food and drink.

Opening Times

- Most shops are open Monday to Saturday from around 10 to 1:30 and 4:30–8.
- Some shops close on Saturday afternoon and most are closed on Sundays.
- The larger department stores and shopping malls in Las Palmas stay open all day, while many shops in the south coast resorts are open daily 10–10.

Top Tips

- It is usual to **bargain** at markets and duty-free shops, where the price quoted may be about double what the shopkeeper is prepared to accept.
- Major **credit cards** are widely accepted.
- The **airport departure lounge** has an extensive shopping mall which is open throughout the night for last-minute purchases, though prices here are no better than elsewhere.

Canarian Classics

- For a good selection of **Canarian crafts** at reasonable prices, check out the Fedac shops in Las Palmas and Playa del Inglés.
- Local handicrafts are also available at the weekly **markets** which take place in various towns around the island.
- **Baskets and basketware** made out of woven palm fronds and banana leaves are manufactured in Ingenio and Teror.
- **Embroidered lace tablecloths** with geometric patterns are a speciality of Ingenio, Agüimes and San Bartolomé de Tirajana. They are sold at markets across the island and at the Museo de Piedras y Artesanía (handicrafts museum) in Ingenio.
- The bone-handled knives known as *naifes* were originally used by shepherds and workers in the banana plantations, but these days they have become a collector's item. Some of the patterns are remarkably intricate, with goathorn handles inlaid with brass. They are made in Santa Maria de Guía and sold in the Fedac shops in Las Palmas and Playa del Inglés.
- **Pottery** is still produced on Gran Canaria without the use of a wheel, just as it was in Guanche times (➤ 13). The main centres of production are La Atalaya, Hoya de Pineda and Lugarejos. In addition to everyday items such as ceramic bowls, jugs and plates, you can buy miniature versions of Guanche artefacts such as the Idol of Tara and jewellery based on the unique *pintaderas* (terracotta seals with geometric designs).
- Traditional **musical instruments** include the *timple* (a small four- or five-stringed guitar) and *chácaras* (castanets).
- If you want to take home some **Canarian music**, the best-known Canarian folk groups are Los Gofiones and Mestisay from Gran Canaria and Los Sabandeños from Tenerife.
- Other **popular souvenirs** include Canarian felt hats and miniature versions of Canarian wooden balconies.
- **Foods** which travel well include palm honey, *bienmesabe* (almond syrup), *mazapan* (almond cake), banana and cactus jam, dried herbs, almonds and jars of spicy *mojo* sauce (➤ 22).
- Other good buys are **coffee beans** from Agaete, **Canarian wine**, Arucas **rum**.
- Cuban-style **cigars** are produced on the nearby island of La Palma and are widely available on Gran Canaria.
- For something more healthy, **soap, shampoo and various skin lotions** are all produced on Gran Canaria from the juice of the aloe vera plant, which claims miraculous healing properties.

Best...
...for cheese:
Santiago Gil Romero, Santa Maria de Guía (▶ 99)
...for pastries:
Dulcería Nublo, Tejeda (▶ 118)
...for wine:
Bodeguilla Juananá, Puerto de Mogán (▶ 146)

Markets

- The two main **food markets** of Las Palmas, Mercado de Vegueta (▶ 61) and Mercado Central (▶ 70) are open Monday to Saturday from 6:30am to 2pm, as are the daily **covered markets** in Arucas and Gáldar.
- The following **weekly markets** offer a varied selection of fresh produce, local crafts, souvenirs, cheap clothes and household goods. Most of them start early and wind up by 2pm.
- Arguineguín (Tue/Thu)
- Arucas (Sat)
- Gáldar (Thu)
- Puerto de Mogán (Fri)
- San Bartolomé de Tirajana (Sun)
- San Fernando (Wed/Sat)
- San Nicolás de Tolentino (Sun)
- Santa Brígida (Sat/Sun)
- Teror (Sun)
- Vecindario (Mon/Wed)
- Vega de San Mateo (Sat/Sun)

Entertainment

Whatever your taste in entertainment, there is always something happening in Gran Canaria. Las Palmas has a thriving arts and music scene, there are hundreds of discos and bars on the south coast, and there is always a local festival taking place somewhere on the island. In addition, hotels and tour operators in all the main resorts lay on a host of entertainments to keep their clients amused. The best sources of information are local newspapers and tourist offices. The weekend editions of *Canarias 7* and *La Provincia* carry full arts and entertainment listings.

Festivals and Folklore

- Traditional *fiestas* on Gran Canaria are colourful affairs. Most of them take place to mark a town or village saint's day, though the Christian element is combined with a heavy dose of pagan ritual dating back to pre-Hispanic times.
- The festivities tend to last for about a **week** and include stick fights, Canarian wrestling competitions (*lucha Canaria*, ▶ 34), bonfires, fireworks, folk dancing, street parties, children's parties, live bands and religious processions.
- **Carnival** (▶ 30) is celebrated across the island, though the biggest parades take place in Las Palmas.
- Details of **other festivals** are listed separately at the end of each chapter. Among the most interesting are Corpus Christi, Las Palmas in June (▶ 72), La Rama, Agaete in August (▶ 100), La Virgen de la Cuevita, Artenara in August (▶ 118), Fiesta del Charco, Puerto de la Aldea in

September (► 149), Nuestra Señora del Rosario, Agüimes in October
(► 149) and the pilgrimage to Nuestra Señora La Virgen del Pino, Teror
in September (► 100).

■ If you cannot get to a festival, you can still see **folk dancing** and hear
Canarian folk music on Sunday at 11:30am at the Pueblo Canario in Las
Palmas (► 70).

Music

■ The main concert venues are the **Auditorio Alfredo Kraus** in Las Palmas,
tel: 928/491-770; www.auditorio-alfredokraus.com (► 71) and
the Las Tirajanas Auditorium in Maspalomas (tel: 928/128-100;
www.maspalomas-congresos.com).

■ There are also various **outdoor music festivals** which take place in
Las Palmas and on the coast. Check with tourist offices for detailed
programmes, and keep an eye out for posters advertising concerts and
special events.

Bars and Clubs

■ The busiest **nightlife** is concentrated in Las Palmas and Playa del Inglés.
Playa del Inglés has a lively gay and lesbian scene, based around the
Yumbo centre (► 148).

■ Nightlife in Gran Canaria starts late and goes on all night. Most **bars** in
Las Palmas and the south coast resorts stay open until 2am, while **discos**
and **clubs** may not close until 6am.

Casinos

■ There are two **casinos** in Gran Canaria. Casino Las Palmas (tel: 928/233-
908; www.casinolaspalmas.com) is in the Hotel Santa Catalina in Las
Palmas (► 66), and Casino Tamarindos Palace (tel: 928/762-724;
www.casinotamarindos) is in the Meliá Tamarindos in San Agustín.

Sport

The mild climate and warm seas make Gran Canaria a paradise for sports
enthusiasts.

Watersports

Conditions for watersports are perfect throughout the year, with sea
temperatures rarely dipping below 19°C (66°F) and reaching an average of
23°C (73°F) in September.

■ **Sailing** and **windsurfing** are best on the south coast, where a number of
schools offer equipment hire and tuition.

■ **Beginners** should stick to the sheltered harbours of the southwest such as
Puerto Rico and Puerto de Mogán, while **experienced** windsurfers enjoy the
challenge of the southeast with its trade winds and strong waves.

■ The **sailing school** at Puerto Rico has produced several Olympic
champions, and the world windsurfing championships have been held in
Gran Canaria. Check out the windsurfing school: Surfcenter Dunkerbeck at
Playa del Águila (tel: 928/762-958; www.dunkerbeck-windsurfing.com).
There's also the excellent Pozo's Centro Internacional de Windsurfing (tel:
928/121-400; www.pozo-ciw.com).

■ To see the **top windsurfers** in action, wait for the summer months, when
the wind speed reaches 60kph (37mph) (Beaufort Scale 7) and the
champion surfers come out to ride the huge waves at Pozo Izquierdo on
the southeast coast.

■ **Surfing** with bodyboards is also popular, especially on Playa de las
Canteras in Las Palmas (► 72) and along the north coast at San Andrés

and Gáldar (➤ 95). In the south, two of the best spots are Playa de las Burras at San Agustín (➤ 159) and Playa de las Mujeres at Maspalomas (➤ 127). Boards can be hired at any of these beaches. The strongest waves are generally between September and March.

- **Scuba diving** is another popular activity, with the chance to see tropical fish, shipwrecks and underwater caves.
- There are fully certified **diving schools** in all the major resorts, with courses for beginners, children over eight years old, and more experienced divers. Most people start in the sheltered harbours of the southwest before moving on to the open sea.
- The best **dive location** on the island is the underwater nature reserve of El Cabrón off the east coast; other good spots are Sardina (➤ 96), La Isleta (Las Palmas) and Pasito Blanco. Some of the diving schools organise excursions to these places.
- If you don't want to scuba dive, most diving schools hire out **snorkelling** equipment.
- **Parascending**, **jet-skiing** and **water-skiing** are among the adrenalin rides on offer at the major south coast resorts. **Pedal boats** are also available for hire and make a good way of getting out on the water with younger children.
- **Swimming** is possible throughout the year because of the warm sea temperature. The beaches of the south coast are generally calm but as this is the Atlantic Ocean, conditions can change rapidly and you need to keep a close eye on children.
- The major **beaches** have lifeguards and safety flags; a red flag indicates that swimming is dangerous.
- Most hotels and apartment blocks have **swimming-pools** and many have a separate pool for children.

Outdoor Activities
- **Fishing** trips can be arranged from the harbour at Puerto Rico (➤ 141), though there is also good rod fishing from the jetties and harbour walls at ports such as Puerto de la Aldea and Puerto de Mogán.
- Fishing in the **inland reservoirs** is only allowed with a licence; for details, enquire at your nearest tourist office.
- **Golf** is growing in popularity, with golfers from northern Europe fleeing frost and winter greens for Gran Canaria's year-round spring climate. There are nine courses on Gran Canaria, the latest by the sea at Meloneras. The oldest golf club in Spain, Real Club de Golf de Las Palmas (➤ 100), is based at Caldera de Bandama and there are also courses at Maspalomas, Las Palmas, Meloneras, Tauro (two), El Salobre and Telde.
- **Walking** in the mountains has been made easier by the restoration of the network of *caminos reales* (royal roads), medieval footpaths which were the main routes across the island. Conditions in the mountains can be very different from on the coast and it is important to be prepared, even in summer, with strong shoes, warm clothing, food, water and a good map.

Spectator Sports
- **Football** is played at the Estadio Insular in Las Palmas, where UD Las Palmas take on Spanish teams in the La Liga between September and June. The most keenly anticipated matches are those against Tenerife.
- *Lucha canaria* (Canarian wrestling) bouts (➤ 35) are held most weeks at arenas across the island. For details, ask at tourist offices or check the fixtures in the local newspapers.
- *Vela Latina* (lateen sailing) regattas take place along the seafront in Las Palmas at weekends between April and October (➤ 72).

Las Palmas

Getting Your Bearings

Crowded, cosmopolitan and teeming with expectation, Las Palmas is the only place in the Canary Islands with that big-city feel. Like any big city, it has its problems with pollution, traffic and crime; but like any big city it also has its compensations, such as good restaurants and shops and a vibrant cultural life. From the museums and historic houses of Vegueta to the bustle of the modern city down by the port, Las Palmas has it all.

Las Palmas stretches out like a long, thin lizard along the island's northeastern tip. The shape of the city has the effect of making it seem even larger than it is; from the old town to the modern centre is a distance of more than 5km (3 miles).

The easiest way to tackle Las Palmas is to break it down into manageable districts, and to travel between them by bus. Head straight for Vegueta, the oldest part, with attractive cobbled streets, shady squares and colonial-style architecture. It was founded by the conqueror Juan Rejón in 1478 on a *vegueta* (meadow) of *las palmas* (palm trees) beside the Guiniguada ravine.

Triana, adjoining Vegueta, has a pleasing mix of buildings from the 16th to 20th centuries, together with theatres, lively shopping streets and open-air bars. North of Parque San Telmo, the long route through various residential districts leads to Parque Santa Catalina, the hub of the modern city. Playa de las Canteras, which must be one of the finest city beaches in the world, is a short walk away. Beyond Puerto de la Luz, Spain's largest port, lie the volcanic peaks of La Isleta, providing a scenic backdrop. Although it is now connected to the mainland by a port built on land reclaimed from the sea, until the 19th century La Isleta was an island, cut off twice a day by high tide.

The distances involved mean this is not really a city for walking, with one magnificent exception – the Avenida Marítima along the seafront. As you stroll along the promenade, with ferries, tankers, cruise ships, navy vessels, yachts and lateen sailboats heading in and out of the port, you appreciate Las Palmas' historic role as a maritime city and a crossroads of continents and cultures.

Preceding page: Yachts in the marina at Las Palmas

Below: Fishing boats on Playa de las Canteras

★ Don't Miss

At Your Leisure

Playa de las Canteras

12

ALP L JONES

11 Museo Elder
10 Parque
Santa Catalina

SANTA
CATALINA

José M Durán

Base
Naval

Puerto
Interior

Club
Náutico

Playa de las Alcaravaneras

ALCARA
VANERAS

Manuel González Martín

Puerto de la Luz

Parque Doramas

9 Pueblo Canario

LUGO

El Caletón

ALTAVISTA

LAS REHOYAS

SAN
NICOLAS

Parque
San Telmo
7

8 Calle Mayor de Triana
CIUDAD DEL MAR

6 Casa Museo Pérez Galdós

REHOYAS
ALTAS

Castillo de
San Francisco

Casa de Colón
Catedral de
Santa Ana

Mercado de
Vegueta

3 4
2 5 Centro Atlántico
de Arte Moderno
(CAAM)

VEGUETA

Museo
Canario
1

| 0 | 500 metres |
| 0 | 500 yards |

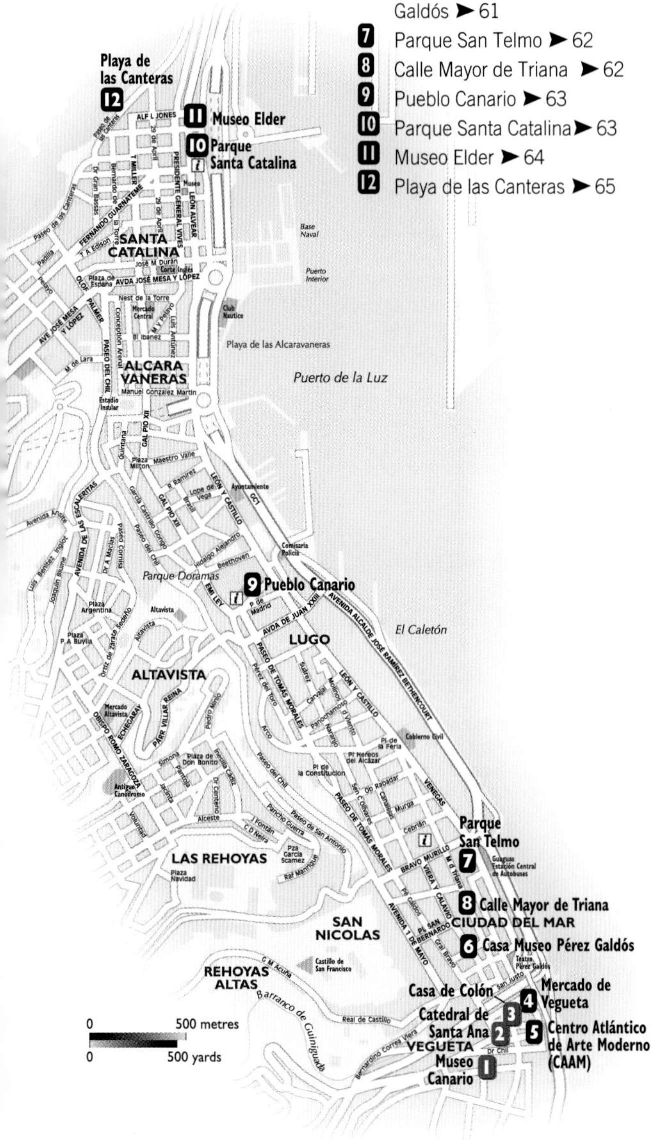

In a Day

If you're not quite sure where to begin your travels, this itinerary recommends a practical and enjoyable day in Las Palmas, taking in some of the best places to see using the Getting Your Bearings map on the previous page. For more information see the main entries

9:00am

Spend some time walking around the Vegueta (below) and soak up the old town atmosphere. Unless it's a Sunday, visit the **4 Mercado de Vegueta** (➤ 61), where the locals do their shopping. Then head for the fascinating **1 Museo Canario** (➤ 52) to learn about the earliest inhabitants of the island, the Guanches.

11:00am

Look into the peaceful courtyard of the **2 Catedral de Santa Ana** (➤ 56; right, view of the city from the cathedral). Follow this with a visit to the **3 Casa de Colón** (➤ 59), where you can explore the history of Las Palmas.

Noon

Go to the **5 Centro Atlantico de Arte Moderno** (➤ 61) to see contemporary art representative of Las Palmas and Canarian life. Then, after all that sightseeing, relax with an apéritif at one of the terrace cafés in Plaza de Cairasco or a spot of window-shopping in the streets around **8 Calle Mayor de Triana** (➤ 62).

1:00pm

Head for **Casa Montesdeoca** (➤ 67) for a lunch-time table in the courtyard. If you feel like something more down-to-earth, **El Herreño** (➤ 67) serves great tapas.

2:30pm

Take a No 1 bus from Parque San Telmo for the journey downtown. On the way, get off at the **9 Pueblo Canario** (➤ 63, above) and a look at this amazing Canarian "village" in the middle of the city. Canarian folk-dancing (above) takes place at 11:30am on Sunday. Hop back on the No 1 bus again and get off at Calle Alfredo L Jones, between **10 Parque Santa Catalina** (➤ 63) and Playa de las Canteras.

4:00pm

Head for Parque Santa Catalina and a ride on the *Guagua Turística* tour bus (➤ 64) before enjoying the hands-on activities at the **11 Museo Elder** (➤ 64) in Parque Santa Catalina. Alternatively, if you feel like you've done enough sightseeing, relax on the beach at **12 Playa de las Canteras** (➤ 63) or take a walk along the promenade.

7:30pm

Take a taxi up to La Isleta for an evening meal at **El Padrino** (➤ 68) and views over the city, with the lights sparkling below.

◻ Museo Canario

If you only see one museum in Gran Canaria, this should be the one. It provides a fascinating introduction to the culture and lifestyle of the earliest Canarios, who have come to be known as the Guanches. As well as glimpses into their daily life, the museum also offers a remarkable collection of complete preserved mummies, whose discovery has provided a link between the Guanches and the ancient Egyptians.

Origins of the Museum

The museum was founded in 1879 by Dr Gregorio Chil, based on his own private collection. At first it was housed in rented premises in the old city hall, but when Dr Chil died in 1901, he bequeathed his collection to the city, along with his home. The museum moved to its present site in 1923, and with the removal of its natural science collection it is now almost totally devoted to archaeology and the lives of the Guanche inhabitants of Gran Canaria between 500 BC and AD 1500.

The exhibits are ranged over 11 galleries on two floors and it makes sense to follow them in order. It is best to allow at least an hour. The first room, **The Habitat**, has scale

THE GUANCHE TRAIL
If the Museo Canario has given you a taste for Guanche culture and history, you can learn more by visiting these sights:
- Barranco de Guayadeque (▶ 124)
- Cenobio de Valerón (▶ 86)
- Cuatro Puertas (▶ 92)
- Mundo Aborigen (▶ 138)
- Roque Bentaiga (▶ 108)

reproductions of Guanche dwellings, including a stone house from Telde and a cave village. Although the Guanches are popularly thought of as cave-dwellers, they actually lived in a variety of houses, including natural caves, artificial caves and stone-built houses that had stone or thatched roofs.

Passing through a small corridor devoted to stonework, where tools such as axes and millstones are displayed, next is a gallery dedicated to the **Guanche economy**. The aboriginal people kept pigs and goats, grew and ground barley, harvested shellfish and made jewellery out of conch shells, all of which is brought to life through a series of realistic tableaux.

The next room is devoted to **magic and religion**, two areas of Guanche culture which are unlikely ever to be fully understood. The accounts of the first invaders suggest that the Guanches worshipped a deity called Alcorán, and that their religion centred on rain-making and fertility. This is reinforced by some of the idols in this room, vivid terracotta figures incorporating human and animal features with explicit depictions of female genitalia. The best-known is the **Idol of Tara**, a red ochre figure with exaggerated breasts, possibly symbolising the earth goddess.

The geometric designs which were widely used by the Guanches may also have had a religious function, with circles representing the sun and triangles the earth, sea and sky. Here also is a reproduction of the *Cueva Pintada* (Painted Cave) at **Gáldar** (➤ 95), with red and black murals of geometric shapes such as circles, spirals, triangles, zigzags and squares. There is also a large collection of *pintaderas*, terracotta or wooden seals with intricate geometric motifs which may have decorated the skin like a tattoo, or painted property as a mark of ownership.

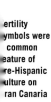

Archaeologists are searching for links between the Guanches and ancient Egyptians

Upper Galleries

The second floor displays begin on the **balcony**, with clothing and other objects made out of leather and vegetable fibres. The tanning of goatskin and pigskin was clearly advanced, and the Guanches also wove intricate baskets and mats out of palm fronds, just as the people of Gran Canaria do today.

Just off from here is the most compelling and macabre section, dealing with **death and mummification** – a practice which the Guanches may have learned from the

Fertility symbols were a common feature of pre-Hispanic culture on Gran Canaria

ancient Egyptians. When Guanche people died, their bodies were washed in the sea, their internal organs were removed and the corpse was left to dry in the sun. It was then wrapped in a shroud made of leather or rush matting and placed inside a cave on planks of wood so that it did not come into contact with the earth. One of the galleries features a reproduction burial cave, and several complete mummies are on display. Some of the mummies are 1.83m (6 feet) tall, reinforcing the idea that the Guanches were an exceptionally tall race.

The walls of this gallery are lined with rows of **Cro-Magnon skulls**. A few of them are shown to have survived a primitive form of trepanning, a surgical operation in which incisions were made in the skull to treat victims of battle injuries and diseases such as epilepsy.

The final galleries feature examples of **pre-Hispanic pottery** and its links to pottery-making techniques on Gran Canaria today. The pottery was made without the use of a potter's wheel, using bones, shells and bamboo sticks to shape the clay. Once again the familiar geometric shapes appear, painted in red ochre to create striking patterns. Similar pieces of pottery are still being produced in the village of La Atalaya (➤ 79) and can be purchased there.

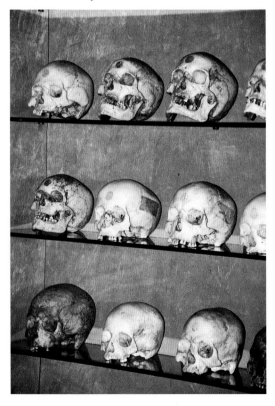

The rows of skulls make a grisly sight

The exterior of the museum

Luigi de Cadamosto, a Venetian explorer, said in 1455: "The sons of Gran Canaria are cunning sharp, they can leap over wide abysses with the greatest of agility and can throw a stone with such sure aim that they never miss the target."

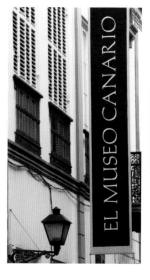

TAKING A BREAK

After leaving the museum stroll down to Calle Mendizábel 20 for coffee, tea, juice, or to the **Tea and Coffee Pot**, not far from the Mercado Vegueta, for a light snack.

🞢 186 C1
✉ Calle Dr Verneau 2
☎ 928/336-800;
www.elmuseocanario.com
🕐 Mon–Fri 10–8, Sat–Sun 10–2
🚌 1 to Teatro Pérez Galdós; 2, 3 to Alameda de Colón
💶 Inexpensive

Replica of a painted cave found at Galdar

MUSEO CANARIO: INSIDE INFO

Top tips The captions are all in Spanish, but the museum shop sells a guidebook with English translations. There are **guided tours** in Spanish that take place at 1, 6 and 7 in summer and 1, 5 and 6 in winter.
- The **shop** sells a good selection of books about the Canary Islands and also has Guanche-related artefacts. The most popular item is a pottery reproduction of the Idol of Tara.

Hidden gem Don't miss the collection of **old maps** in the reading room, some of which date back to the time of Columbus.

In more depth The museum has a **library and historical archive** containing more than 40,000 items. It is open Monday to Friday 10–8.

2 Catedral de Santa Ana

The largest church in the Canary Islands dominates the Vegueta skyline and looks down over a handsome square from its impressive neo-classical façade. Begun in 1497, it took more than 400 years to complete, with the result that it is a curious and eclectic blend of Gothic, Renaissance, baroque and neo-classical styles.

The Courtyard

Unless you are arriving for a service, you will enter through the **Patio de los Naranjos** (Courtyard of the Orange Trees), just around the corner from the main entrance on the square. This beautiful cloister is built in late 16th-century Canarian style and has wooden galleries along two of its sides. Notice the ceramic plaque dedicated to the bishops of the Canary Islands who have served in America, an indication of the close links between the Canaries and Spain's Latin American colonies over the past 500 years.

Also in the courtyard, the **Museo Diocesano** (Diocesan Museum) is devoted to religious art. A staircase leads to the **Sala Capitular** (chapter-house), with a hand-made ceramic tiled floor, unique in the Canary Islands, and sculptures by Luján Pérez (a well-known Canarian artist). The other galleries have paintings and furniture, including an 18th-century throne by Canarian goldsmith José Eugenio.

Below: The Patio de los Naranjos

The cathedral has been restored to its former glory

Airy interior

A 16th-century doorway, Puerta del Aire, leads to the **main cathedral**. After a recent restoration, the interior is full of light and space, and the grey basalt columns of the original Gothic structure are shining once again. There are three naves of equal height, and side chapels containing the tombs of various bishops, as well as the poet Bartolomé Cairasco (1538–1610), the historian José de Viera y Clavijo (1731–1813) and the diplomat Fernando de León y Castillo (1842–1918), whose grandiloquent tomb lists his many titles and records his wish to be buried among his people in Gran Canaria. The figures of saints beneath the dome were sculpted by Luján Pérez, the artist responsible for remodelling the cathedral's façade in the 19th century.

Vantage Point

A separate ticket gives access to the **cathedral tower**. A lift takes you up to the viewing platform but you can climb to the top of the tower for even better views. From here you look down over Plaza de Santa Ana, the main square of the old town, with its bronze dogs, lampstands, palm trees and Renaissance mansions.

During the **feast of Corpus Christi** in June (► 72), the Plaza de Santa Ana becomes a carpet of flowers and participants throw rose-petals from their balconies as a procession moves out of the cathedral and around the streets of the old town.

TAKING A BREAK

The pavement cafés of **Plaza de Cairasco** are perfect for people-watching and are a short walk from the cathedral, across the main road which separates Vegueta from Triana.

Climb to the top of the tower for the views

🚩 186 C1
✉ Plaza de Santa Ana (entrance at Calle Espíritu Santo 20)
☎ 928/314-989
🕐 Cathedral: daily 9–8. Museum: Mon–Fri 10–4:30, Sat 10–1:30
🚌 1 to Teatro Pérez Galdós; 2, 3 to Alameda de Colón
💶 Inexpensive

CATEDRAL DE SANTA ANA: INSIDE INFO

Top tip You can get into the cathedral for **free** by going to Mass on Sunday morning – though the museum and Patio de los Naranjos will be off limits.

Hidden gem Look out for the *Stations of the Cross* by Jésus Arencibia, a remarkable series of black-and-white drawings completed in the 1960s and exhibited in the gallery nearest to the courtyard entrance.

One to miss Once you have seen the Sala Capitular, you could afford to miss the rest of the **Museo Diocesano** if you are in a hurry.

③ Casa de Colón

Pass through the heavy doors of one of the oldest houses in Las Palmas and you enter a cool courtyard, with dark wooden balconies surrounding a Renaissance patio and a pair of noisy parrots standing guard over an ancient stone well. If Christopher Columbus ever set foot in Las Palmas then he almost certainly stayed in this house. Most historians agree that he called in at Las Palmas on his way to discover Cuba during his first voyage to the New World in 1492. If so, he would have presented his credentials and been given lodging at the military governor's residence, one of the first buildings to be completed in Las Palmas following the Spanish Conquest of 1478.

Whatever the truth about Columbus, this house, the Casa de Colón (Colón means Columbus to Canarians) is worth a visit as it is one of the finest examples of traditional Canarian architecture, with carved stone portals, balconies and richly ornamented façades. It has been turned into a museum dedicated to Columbus, linking together his voyages, the history of the Canary Islands and their role as a bridge between Europe and America.

Did Christopher Columbus sleep here?

If you only have time for a short visit, the **ground-floor rooms** offer the most interesting material on Columbus and his voyages. Among the nautical charts, navigational instruments and model boats, look out for the following:

- a faithful reconstruction of the **poop deck** of Columbus' ship *La Niña*.
- the **log book** of Columbus' first voyage to the New World, with an entry recording how he called in at Las Palmas for repairs to his ship
- the **seals of the Treaty of Tordesillas** (1494), which divided the undiscovered Atlantic into Spanish and Portuguese spheres of influence
- the **map** of the known world in 1500 drawn by Spanish cartographer Juan de la Cosa, who accompanied Columbus on his early voyages, which included those parts of America discovered by Columbus but missed out large parts of the continent.

The **upstairs galleries** contain exhibits on the history of Las Palmas as well as a collection of 16th- to 20th-century paintings on loan from the Prado Museum in Madrid.

Above: Children enjoy the model ships and medieval maps

TAKING A BREAK

For lunch, try the Canarian tapas at **El Herreño** (➤ 67) or the grand surroundings of **Casa Montesdeoca** (➤ 67) for Canarian cuisine.

➕ 186 C1 ✉ Calle Colón 1 ☎ 928/312-373 ◉ Mon–Fri 9–7, Sat–Sun 9–3
🚌 1 to Teatro Pérez Galdós; 2, 3 to Alameda de Colón 💷 Free

CASA DE COLÓN: INSIDE INFO

Hidden gem The **crypt** is devoted to objects from the pre-Colombian period, showing the richness of the various American cultures before he arrived. Among the artefacts on display are Ecuadorean fertility symbols dating back to 500 BC, replicas of Aztec and Mayan pottery, and basketware from the 20th-century "pre-Colombian" Yanomani Indians of Brazil.

One to miss If you are in a hurry, the **Prado collection** contains little that is exceptional, apart from some etchings by Goya and a *Virgin and Child* by Luis de Menéndez.

At Your Leisure

④ Mercado de Vegueta

A visit to Las Palmas' oldest market is a good way to appreciate the variety of fresh produce available on Gran Canaria. This is where the locals do their shopping and it is busy from early in the morning. Stalls around the outer aisles sell Atlantic fish such as *sama* and *cherne* as well as octopus, squid and sole. Greengrocers sell local bananas, tomatoes, potatoes, mangoes, avocados and figs. Other stalls specialise in Canarian cheeses, such as *queso de flor* from Guía and goat's cheese from Fuerteventura, with its paprika-coated rind.

All around the market are stand-up tapas bars and *churrerias*, where people come after doing their shopping to dip *churros* (dough fritters) into mugs of coffee or chocolate – don't miss Churreria Mayda, which has been making *churros* since 1948. The market used to be known as the "market of the forty thieves", ostensibly because of the number of stalls.

✚ 186 C1 ✉ Corner of Plaza del Mercado and Calle Mendizábal ⓞ Mon–Thu 6:30–2, Fri, Sat 6:30–3 🚍 1 to Teatro Pérez Galdós

⑤ Centro Atlántico de Arte Moderno (CAAM)

Step behind the 18th-century façade of a typical old Vegueta house and you enter this bright, modern art museum, with sparkling white walls and a glass-covered rooftop terrace. Opened in 1989, the museum has become a focal point of contemporary cultural life in Las Palmas. There is a rolling programme of temporary exhibitions, but the emphasis is on Canarian art and the relationship between the Atlantic cultures of Europe, Africa and America. The museum has a separate gallery in Plaza de San Antonio Abad, near the Casa de Colón, which acts as a showcase for exhibitions of work by young Canarian artists.

✚ 186 C1 ✉ Calle de los Balcones 9–11 ☎ 928/311-824; www. caam.net ⓞ Tue–Sat 10–9, Sun 10–2 🚍 1 to Teatro Pérez Galdós; 2, 3 to Alameda de Colón 🎟 Free

⑥ Casa Museo Pérez Galdós

This typical Canarian, 18th-century home was the birthplace of Benito Pérez Galdós (1843–1920), the Canary Islands' greatest novelist and a leading exponent of Spanish Realism who has been compared to Balzac and Dickens. His best-known work is *Episodios Nacionales*, a vivid portrait of 19th-century Spain. Although he left Las Palmas at the age of 19 and never returned, the islanders are extremely proud of Pérez Galdós and the house has been turned into a museum devoted to his life and work. It contains mementoes of his life from his cradle (he was the youngest of ten children) to his death mask, as well as manuscripts, furniture and reproductions of his bedroom and study from Madrid and Santander. Don't miss the statue

A breakfast of soft *churros* with a cup of hot chocolate

of Pérez Galdós in the courtyard – a copy of which stands on top of the bus station in Parque San Telmo.

➕ 186 C1 ✉ Calle Cano 2–6 ☎ 928/366-976; www.casamuseoperezgaldos.com 🕐 Mon–Fri 10–2, 4–8, Sat, Sun 10–2 (tours on the hour) 🚌 1, 11 to Parque San Telmo 💷 Free

🟥 Parque San Telmo

The most appealing of all Las Palmas' parks, this is the one most people see first as they step out of the bus station. There are palm trees giving shade, benches and a playground, but the main attractions are the bandstand in the middle and the Modernist (Spanish art nouveau) café inside a pavilion decorated with ceramic tiles. The park was initially built on the site of a small cove but the bus station and motorway have forced the sea to recede. The chapel in the southwest corner is dedicated to sailors and fishermen, with model boats hanging from the ceiling.

Near here is the military headquarters where General Franco

A Modernist façade to a café in Parque San Telmo

launched the Civil War in 1936; a plaque marks the spot where he announced his rebellion "for the salvation of Spain".

➕ 186 C2 🚌 1, 11

🟥 Calle Mayor de Triana

This was the first street in Las Palmas to be pedestrianised in the 1970s and it has become a popular place to take a stroll. The best time to come

FOUR TOP MONUMENTS
- Sculpture of Guanche pole vaulter, in the gardens of the Hotel Santa Catalina (▶ 66)
- Bust of Christopher Columbus, Alameda de Colón
- Monument to Pérez Galdós, Plaza de la Feria
- Monument to Canarian farmers, Plaza de España

is during the early-evening *paseo*
(around 6–8), when people spill on
to the streets and street musicians
entertain the crowds.

Until quite recently Las Palmas'
principal shopping street, it is most
notable for its range of architectural
styles, with several shopfronts in
Modernist (Spanish art nouveau)
style. Although the biggest stores
have now moved elsewhere, this
is still a pleasant area for shopping
or simply browsing, with craft
shops and arty boutiques in the
surrounding streets.

➕ 186 C2 🚌 1, 11 to Parque San Telmo

🟦 Pueblo Canario

This "village" of traditional Canarian
buildings in the heart of a modern
city may seem like a tourist trap,
but it was designed as
exactly the opposite,
a serious attempt to
preserve Canarian
culture and architecture
before tourism wiped
them out. There is
nothing artificial about
the enthusiastic displays
of folk dancing, which
take place on Sunday
mornings in front of an
appreciative and largely
Spanish audience. The
women wear white
bodices and long
flowing dresses, the men
embroidered waistcoats,
white skirts and socks
around the knees, and
the songs vary from
jaunty to melancholy,
with a strong hint of
the Caribbean.

The complex was
designed by the

Modernist artist Néstor Martín
Fernández de la Torre (1887–1938),
whose work is on display in the
Museo Néstor. Among the highlights
are his epic cycles *Poema del Atlántico*
(*Atlantic Poem*), in which the sea is
interwoven with scenes from ancient
mythology, and the unfinished *Poema
de la Tierra* (*Earth Poem*), blending
themes of erotic love with studies of
native Canarian plants.

➕ 186 B3 ✉ Parque Doramas 🕙 Folk
dancing: Sun 11:30am 🚌 1 💷 Free (Café
and restaurant moderate)

Museo Néstor
➕ 186 B3 ☎ 928/245-135 🕙 Tue–Fri 10–8,
Sun 10:30–2:30 💷 Inexpensive

🔟 Parque Santa Catalina

This large open space, more like
a plaza than a park, is the nearest
thing this sprawling city has to a
centre. With cafés, news-stands,
playgrounds and shops, the square
is busy day and night. This is where

**The folk dancing displays at the Pueblo
Canario are always popular – get there
early if you want a seat**

FOR KIDS
The top family attraction is the
Museo Elder (➤ 64), though older
children might enjoy the model
boats at the **Casa de Colón** (➤ 59)
and the rows of ghoulish skulls and
the mummies at the **Museo Canario**
(➤ 52). There are **playgrounds** in all
the parks, and the beach at **Playa
de las Canteras** (➤ 65) is very child-
friendly. The rides on the open-top
Guagua Turística (➤ 38) are also
ideal for children.

go inside a F5 plane, explore the
properties of sound and waves, and
learn about energy. Look out for the
fascinating Betancourt machine at
the entrance to the museum – it
never stops!

The most fun to be had is on
the first floor, with exhibits relating
to mathematics, magnetism and
the human body. You can move
pieces around a chess set, solve
mathematical riddles, blow up a hot-
air balloon and work out what your
weight would be on the moon before
coming to grips with the world's
largest magic square.

Adults and older children may
also enjoy the ground-floor displays
on transport and astronomy, with
cars and planes to test out. An area
is devoted to temporary exhibitions
covering a further range of subjects

**The locals gather to play chess at the
café tables in Parque Santa Catalina**

you can most feel the cosmopolitan
atmosphere of Las Palmas, as tourists
mingle with sailors, shoeshine boys,
hustlers, African traders, and the
elderly men who play dominoes
and chess beneath the palm trees.
Just across the road from here cruise
ships docked in the port are a
prominent sight, alongside
the La Muelle shopping
and entertainment
complex.

The plaza is also home
to the popular Museo Elder
and the starting-point for
the *Guagua Turística* tour
bus (➤ 38).
186 A5 **1, 2, 3**

Museo Elder
The slogan of this science
museum, which opened in
1999, is "*Tocar por favor*"
("Please do touch"). Of
more than 200 exhibits,
all but a handful are
interactive and visitors are
encouraged to pull levers
and push buttons to their
hearts' content. All exhibits
are labelled in English as
well as Spanish, making
this is a great place to
take the children, but be
warned that those with
an inquisitive nature may
never want to leave. Here
you can also watch chicks
hatch from their eggs,

Looking across the promenade behind
Playa de las Canteras

such as "Flying: 100 years on
air" and "Wings and machines".
Education is vital to this museum but
fun and interaction are not forgotten.

There is also a large-screen
IMAX cinema which shows films
in English, and an open-air terrace
café offers views over Parque Santa
Catalina to enjoy with your coffee.

🚹 186 A5 ✉ Parque Santa Catalina
☎ 828/011-828; www.museoelder.org
🕐 Tue–Sun 10–8 in winter (Jul–end Aug 11–9)
🚌 1, 2, 3, 12, 30, 32, 42 💵 Moderate (IMAX
cinema extra)

🔟 Playa de las Canteras

The popular Playa de las Canteras
offers more than 3km (2 miles) of
golden sand set in a sheltered bay
and protected by a natural rock
barrier which breaks the waves and
turns the sea into a warm, shallow
lagoon at low tide.

Long before the south coast
was developed, this was the first
tourist resort in Gran Canaria, and
the bucket-and-spade atmosphere
survives, along the wide promenade,

with its ice-cream parlours, beach
shops and Italian cafés.

At the western end of the beach,
where the reef runs out, surfers ride
the waves in front of the Auditorio
Alfredo Kraus, a mosque-like
building constructed out of volcanic
rock by the Catalan architect Oscar
Tusquets. The auditorium, which
opened in 1997, is named after
the Canarian tenor Alfredo Kraus
(1927–99), who gave one of his last
recitals here.

🚹 186 A5 🚌 1, 2, 3, 20, 21

LA ISLETA
The steep volcanic terrain and barren
landscape of this tiny peninsula
mark the northern boundary of Las
Palmas. At the centre of the district
is Plaza Manuel Becerra, a lively
square with a lighthouse on one side
and the harbour gate on the other.
Narrow streets with street vendors,
shops and bars surround the square.
La Isleta is very popular with surfers
and offers great views over the city,
and is also an important naval base.

Where to... Stay

Prices

The symbols refer to the average cost of a double room in high season, generally November to April. All prices exclude 4.5 per cent sales tax (IGIC).

€ under €70 **€€** €70–€130 **€€€** over €130

The majority of hotels in Las Palmas are gathered around Las Canteras beach but still ideal for visiting the city sights; to get the most out of your stay, pay the extra for a balcony room with sea view. Start the day with a good buffet breakfast served overlooking the ocean. The hotel is particularly well fitted out for those with disabilities. There are nice touches like free beach towels.
186 off map at A5 ✉ **Calle Portugal**
🕿 **928/224–062; www.hotelsdunas.com**

Dunas Canteras €€

At the quieter end of Las Canteras beach but still ideal for visiting the city sights; to get the most out of your stay, pay the extra for a balcony room with sea view. Start the day with a good buffet breakfast served overlooking the ocean. The

Madrid €

For those who put character before comfort, this rambling old colonial hotel on one of Las Palmas' most attractive squares is just about the only place to stay. The antique furniture and old-style wooden beds have probably been in place since 1936, when General Franco spent his last night here before launching the Spanish Civil War. Ask for a room with a balcony over the square (it can get noisy at night).
186 C1 ✉ **Plaza de Cairasco 4**
🕿 **928/360-664**

Parque €€

This hotel facing Parque San Telmo is convenient for the old town and makes a good base for excursions around the island as the bus station is just one minute away. The rooms are comfortable and modern and some of them have views over the park. There are more good views from the top-floor restaurant and the rooftop sun terrace. This is the best choice in Las Palmas in the medium price bracket.
186 C2 ✉ **Muelle de Las Palmas 2**
🕿 **928/368-000; www.hparque.com**

Reina Isabel €€€

The best of the hotels on Las Canteras beach has been thoroughly modernised and is a stylish place to stay. The rooftop pool is ideal for soaking up the sun and the hotel has private sunbeds and parasols on the beach. The top-floor restaurant features modern Spanish cuisine, and a beachside terrace café has sandwiches and snacks. Most rooms have balconies overlooking the sea.
186 A5 ✉ **Calle Alfredo L Jones 40**
🕿 **928/260-100; www.bullhotels.com/es/reinaisabel**

Santa Catalina €€€

Royalty and heads of state have stayed in this old-world hotel, which first opened in 1890. Dark wooden balconies look down over tropical gardens, and the wicker chairs on the veranda are a good place for cocktails or afternoon tea. Facilities include a pool and spa centre, casino and a daily courtesy bus to the beach, 2km (1 mile) away. Parque Doramas behind the hotel, is a peaceful place for a stroll.
186 B3 ✉ **Calle León y Castillo 227** 🕿 **928/243-040;**
www.hotelsantacatalina.com

Where to...
Eat and Drink

Prices
Expect to pay per person for a meal, excluding drinks and service
€ under €15   €€ €15–€30   €€€ over €30

Most restaurants on Gran Canaria are open throughout the year, though they may close at some time during the year for an annual holiday.

Café Santa Catalina €
This pleasant, open-air café is on Las Palmas' central square, where elderly men gather to play chess and dominoes beneath the palms. With wicker chairs on a shady terrace, it makes a good place to while away some time reading the papers, writing your postcards or just watching the world go by. The lunch menu is Italian-influenced, featuring pasta, pizza and salads, but most people just come for an ice-cream or a coffee and a pastry.
🕀 186 A5 ⊠ Parque Santa Catalina
🕐 Daily 9am–1am

Casa Carmelo €€€
With a wonderful view over the bay at Playa de Las Canteras, this restaurant at the north end of the beach serves meats from Uruguay and Argentina grilled in barbecue style. If you prefer fish you will find some good fresh options. The outside terrace has great views of the sea and the large inside restaurant is pleasantly decorated with typical Canarian wooden ceiling and yellow walls. The service is good and friendly.
🕀 186 A5 ⊠ Paseo de Las Canteras 2
🕐 928/469-056 🕐 Daily 1–4:30, 7:30–12:30

Casa Montesdeoca €€€
The most elegant restaurant in Las Palmas is housed in a 16th-century town house, built by the Jewish Montes de Oca family, who gave their name to the street. The bar, with its old portraits and hanging hams, is a good place to meet but you should try to get a table on the patio. The service is formal and over-attentive at times, but the cooking is first-class. The menu has Canarian and Spanish dishes with an emphasis on fish, and there is a good selection of both local and Spanish wines.
🕀 186 C1 ⊠ Calle Montesdeoca 10
🕐 928/333-466 🕐 Mon–Sat 12:30–4, 8–midnight

El Herreño €–€€
Hanging hams in the bar and a large brick oven give this place a rustic feel, enhanced by the buzz of conversation and the bustle of the white-shirted waiters. It is in the courtyard of an old house just around the corner from the Mercado de Vegueta. The owner is from El Hierro, one of the Canary Islands, and so naturally the menu features traditional Canary Islands cooking, accompanied by local wine. The house special is a delicious dish of roast pork with a handful of roast potatoes, which makes an excellent lunch-time snack. Also serves good tapas.
🕀 186 C1 ⊠ Calle Mendizábal 5
🕐 928/310-555 🕐 Daily 9:30am–1am

El Novillo Precoz €€€
Transport yourself to the plains of Uruguay. The ephemera displayed here conjures up cattle – some of the photographs on the wall feature once-living beasts – and gauchos, the items on the walls are

those used in the round up. This is a meat-eater's heaven with beef flown in three times a week to be flash-grilled on the open fire. It's an upmarket restaurant that boasts some ten types of different steak dishes. The accompanying salads and side dishes bring a Canarian flavour to your meal. Bring only carnivorous dining companions.

186 off map at A5 ⊠ Calle Portugal 9 ☎ 928/221-659; www.novillosprecoz.com ⊙ Tue–Sun 1–4, 8–midnight

El Padrino €€

Drive to the end of the road on La Isleta – or take bus 41 – to reach this celebrated fish restaurant. The people of Las Palmas come here for a good thing when they see one. Most of the tables are out of doors, in a large greenhouse beside the car-park which can get stiflingly hot in summer. The crusty bread comes straight out of the oven and is served with a bowl of allioli (garlic mayonnaise). Almost everything on the menu is fishy, including seafood flown in from Galicia as well as the local catch. The menu contains a list of the day's suggestions and it is probably worth heeding their advice.

181 D5 ⊠ Calle Jesús Nazareno 1, Las Coloradas ☎ 928/462-094 ⊙ Daily 8–11

Hotel Madrid €

The tables on the square outside this historic hotel (▶ 66) are the perfect place for an early-evening drink, accompanied by a plate of papas arrugadas (spicy potatoes) or pork crackling rolled in gofio. Although most people come here for a snack before moving on elsewhere, the bar also serves reasonably priced set meals at lunchtime and in the evening. Brothers Vladimir and Paco, who own the hotel, will keep you laughing while they're serving your meal.

186 C1 ⊠ Plaza de Cairasco 4 ☎ 928/360-664 ⊙ Daily noon–midnight

La Cava Triana €–€€

This restaurant/wine bar is on a quiet street. The interior is a stylish mix of traditional and modern with maroon walls hung with engravings, plus wooden tables and chairs. The Spanish menu features meat dishes such as lamb with caramelised onions and the desserts are modernised versions of the classics such as bienmesabe, the local almond cream pudding. There is a fine selection of Riojas and other good Spanish choices.

186 C1 ⊠ Calle Travieso 35 ☎ 928/381-302 ⊙ Mon–Sat 12.30pm–1:30am

La Marinera €€–€€€

Dine close to the beach at the north end of Playa de Las Canteras, either on the terrace or in the air-conditioned restaurant with panoramic views of the bay. La Marinera offers an excellent choice of starters, local fresh fish – you can look at the fish on offer before you make your decision – and seafood paella. A speciality of the house is the marinaded tuna. There is also a good selection of grilled meats.

186 A5 ⊠ Paseo de la Canteras, Plaza la Puntilla ☎ 928/468-802 ⊙ Daily noon–midnight

La Pasta Real €€

An excellent Italian restaurant that has been owned by the Blanco Cornejo family for more than 20 years. Two small rooms are decorated with frescoes of Italian landscapes, and the family provides excellent home-cooking. One of the few restaurants in town to cater for vegetarians, it includes macrobiotic specialities. For meat eaters there are filet steaks and succulent lamb. Specialities include endive and Roquefort pastry, fresh salmon or sirloin carpaccio, lettuce hearts stuffed with tuna pasta and meat pasticcio (like lasagne). Leave room for one of the original desserts.

186 off map at A4 ⊠ Calle Secretario Padilla 28 ☎ 928/262-267 ⊙ Daily 1–4, Mon, Wed–Sat 8–midnight. Closed two weeks in May

Where to... Shop

The focus of shopping in Las Palmas has gradually shifted away from the old town and towards the port.

The **specialist** shops are still to be found in Vegueta and in the streets around Calle Mayor de Triana, but the **upmarket fashion boutiques** have moved downtown to the smarter Avenida Mesa y López district.

Between here and the port, the area around Parque Santa Catalina resembles an **Oriental bazaar**, with Indian-run shops selling inexpensive cameras, watches, cigars, clothes and electronic goods on streets such as Calle Tomás Miller, Calle Luis Morote and Calle Alfredo L Jones.

SHOPPING CENTRES

The local people do their shopping at the huge **shopping** centres which sprang up on the edge of the city in the 1990s. These giant malls are a mixture of shopping and entertainment, with multiplex cinemas, restaurants and pubs open well into the night.

The biggest centre is **La Ballena**, 3km (2 miles) out of town on the road to Teror. This has a hypermarket and more than 100 shops, including many well-known names. A second shopping centre, **Las Arenas**, is situated at the west end of Las Canteras beach, facing the Auditorio Alfredo Kraus and close to one of the stops for the *Guagua Turística* tour bus.

The latest centre is El Nivelle, smaller but more chic in a glass building at Puerto de la Luz. It features well-known international and Spanish chain stores.

AVENIDA MESA Y LÓPEZ

This wide avenue, with a charming laurel-shaded promenade at its centre, is the principal shopping street of Las Palmas. At the top of the promenade, **Plaza de España** (also known as Plaza de la Victoria) is a busy roundabout with a monument at its centre, dedicated to Canarian farmers and mothers.

This popular meeting-place is where supporters of **UD Las Palmas** football team gather to celebrate their team's victories.

Department Store

This is where you will find **El Corte Inglés**, the biggest department store on the island, with two branches on opposite sides of the street. The main store, on the

northern side, has four floors of fashions for women, men, children and teenagers, a supermarket in the basement and the **Club del Gourmet**, featuring Canarian and Spanish food and wines. There's a top floor café and a more substantial restaurant. The second shop across the street sells **books, music, electronic goods, household items and souvenirs**. Both stores are open Monday to Saturday, 10–10.

Fashion and Designer Boutiques

The rest of Avenida Mesa y López is mostly devoted to fashion and designer boutiques. Among the well-known names here are **Benetton** (two branches), **Massimmo Dutti** (fashion), **López** (shoes and leather goods), **Zara** (both home and fashion), **Don Juan** (shoes and accessories), **Mango** (fashion), **Cortefiel** (department store) and **Marks & Spencer** (department store).

TRIANA

Calle Mayor de Triana (▶ 62) is no longer the main shopping street in town, but it is still the best place for a paseo combined with a spot of window-shopping and has been accurately maintained with floral displays. There are one or two high-street names here, such as **Benetton** and **Zara**, but it is the quirky shops in the side streets which give this area its appeal. Locally made goods are available in most of the shops mentioned below.

When you feel like a break from shopping, there are several pavement cafés along Calle Mayor, where you might be entertained by the nearby street musicians.

Books

La Librería del Cabildo Insular (Calle Cano 24) is a bookshop run by the Gran Canarian government, with a wide range of books on Gran Canaria as well as walking maps and Canarian music on CD.

Crafts

Also worth seeking out is **Fedac** (Calle Domingo J Navarro 7, a government-sponsored craft shop which sells goods direct from the producers at non-profit prices. Among the items are pottery, basketware, lace, bone-handled knives, jewellery, musical instruments and mini Canarian balconies. **Atarecos** (Calle Cano 30) stocks local handicrafts as well as Latin American clothing and jewellery. On Calle Mayor itself, **Natural Selection** is a branch of a well-known chain, at No 92, offering fairly traded goods (silk, cotton, candles, crafts) from around the world, together with New Age books and music. For a souvenir with a difference visit **Orbis** (Calle Major de Triana 51), where you will find off-the-peg and custom-made *timbales*, a small Canarian guitar.

Confectionery

Casa Ricardo (corner of Calle Mayor and Calle Losero) is the confectionery shop of your dreams, with a colourful and tempting pick-and-mix selection which includes strawberry golf balls, orange bonbons, heart-shaped lollipops and peach-flavoured liquorice.

MARKETS

Mercado de Vegueta (▶ 61): this is Las Palmas' oldest, busiest and best food market.

Mercado Central (Calle Galicia): this second food market is situated conveniently close to Avenida Mesa y López.

Mercado del Puerto (Calle Albareda): a covered market down by the port, with more of an international flavour. Seafood and fresh produce are sold inside, and stalls around the edge cater for foreign sailors passing through.

Mercado de las Flores (Plaza de Pilar): arts, crafts and flower market which takes place on Sunday mornings in this attractive old town square.

In **Parque San Telmo** there is a lively flea-market on Sunday morning.

PUEBLO CANARIO

This Canarian-style "village" of traditional architecture (▶ 63) contains souvenir and craft shops where you can buy T-shirts, folk costumes, ceramics, books and Gran Canarian folk music. Traditional folk music accompanies folk-dancing, which you can see in performances on Sunday mornings.

BARGAIN OPTIONS

You can pick up some good bargains as Gran Canaria operates a free-trade policy. For perfume and cosmetics there are chain stores with branches throughout the city, Defa, Maya and Yves Rocher. For electronics try Visanta and visit specialist tobacco shops for cigarettes and cigars (try Juan Marques at Calle Ripoche 1).

Where to...
Be Entertained

MUSIC AND DRAMA

Theatre and concert listings can be found in the daily newspapers *Canarias 7* and *La Provincia*. There are also various English-language newspapers such as the *RTN (Round Town News)*, available from the kiosks in Parque Santa Catalina and aimed firmly at an expatriate readership. If you have internet access, it is worth consulting the daily programme of cultural events on www.canarynet.com, which you can find by clicking on 'agenda' in the left-hand column.

Plays are staged at the Teatro Pérez Galdós, designed by Miguel Martín Fernández de la Torre with murals by his brother Néstor. A favourite haunt of the Las Palmas bourgeoisie, this is once again home to the Las Palmas Philharmonic Society having opened in 2008, after undergoing restoration work. It also hosts opera, highlighting the popular Spanish light opera *zarzuela*.

The other principal theatres are **Teatro Guiniguada** (currently undergoing restoration), on the opposite side of the road which separates Triana from Vegueta, and the Teatro Cuyás, which opened in 2000 in a former cinema in Triana. Look out too for performances at the Cultural Centre and CICCA (Centro de Iniciativas de la Caja de Canarias).

Since its opening in 1997, the **Auditorio Alfredo Kraus** (www.auditorio-alfredokraus.com) on Las Canteras beach has become the main concert venue in the city and the largest performance space in the Canary Islands. The symphony hall holds more than 1,600 people, with a window behind the stage giving spectacular ocean views. In addition to opera and classical music, the auditorium is used for concerts ranging from salsa to Latin jazz.

It is also the principal venue for several major **festivals**, including an international music festival (Jan/Feb), dance and theatre festival (Jul–Aug), Alfredo Kraus Opera Festival (Mar–Jun). It is also one of the venues for the Festival of Jazz held during July. The area facing the auditorium is an open-air concert space, Plaza de la Música.

The **WOMAD** (World of Music, Arts and Dance) festival takes place in November in Parque Santa Catalina. Free events feature musicians from around the world. Canarian folk music and dancing take place once a week at the Pueblo Canario (▶ 63, 70).

FILMS

The latest international blockbusters dubbed into Spanish, as well as contemporary Spanish films, are shown at multiplex cinemas around the city. The biggest are in the Las Arenas, La Ballena and El Muelle shopping centres, though the Royal and Monopol cinemas are convenient options in the centre of town. Full listings can be found in the local newspapers.

An international film festival takes place in end February/March in venues including the Las Arenas multiplex and Auditorio Alfredo Kraus (▶ this page).

NIGHTLIFE

As in the rest of Spain, nightlife starts late and few people would consider going out before 10pm. The "in" places come and go, but as a general rule the old town districts of **Vegueta** and **Triana** have a more sophisticated appeal,

UD Las Palmas football team play host to other Spanish teams, including local rivals Tenerife. Most matches are on Sunday afternoons September to June at the new **Estadio de Gran Canaria** (Fondos de Segura, Lomo de San Lázaro). Tickets for most games are sold on the day of the match.

One sport which is peculiar to Las Palmas is **Vela Latina**, regattas featuring small "lateen" boats with outsize sails and a crew of between eight and 12 people.

Regattas take place most weekends between April and October (on Saturday afternoons and Sunday mornings) to take advantage of the prevailing trade winds. The boats race along the east coast of Las Palmas from Playa de la Laja to Playa de Alcaravaneras. The best vantage points for viewing the races are the Muelle Deportivo marina, or anywhere along the Avenida Marítima promenade.

San Juan (24 Jun): pagan and Christian rituals and a celebration of the founding of Las Palmas. Bonfires are lit on the beaches on the night of 24 Jun, the high point of a week of concerts, theatre, dance and sporting activities.

La Virgen del Carmen (16 Jul): processions of fishing boats in La Isleta and Puerto de la Luz in honour of the Virgin, patron saint of fishermen.

Fiestas de la Naval (6 Oct): La Isleta celebrates the victory of the Spanish Armada over the British explorer Sir Francis Drake in 1595.

Sailing, windsurfing and scuba-diving courses are available at the Muelle Deportivo marina and the Real Club Victoria at the eastern end of Playa de las Canteras. The best place for ordinary surfing is at the western end of Las Canteras, beneath the Auditorio Alfredo Kraus (► 71).

For those who enjoy a flutter, the **Casino Las Palmas** (open Sun–Thu 8pm–4pm, Fri–Sat 8pm–5am) is inside the Hotel Santa Catalina. Blackjack, baccarat and roulette are played here. Men must wear a tie, and you will need a passport.

Día de los Reyes (5 Jan): the eve of Epiphany offers a street parade for the city's children, led by characters playing the Three Wise Men.

Carnival (Feb): the pre-Lenten Carnival celebrations in Las Palmas are the biggest on the island, beginning with the election of the Carnival Queen and continuing with open-air street parties, masked balls and fancy-dress parades.

Semana Santa (Mar/Apr): Holy Week processions with sacred icons and religious sculptures.

Corpus Christi (late May/early Jun): the streets of the old town are decorated with flowers and Plaza de Santa Ana a carpet of floral displays.

while the focus of young nightlife is around **Parque Santa Catalina** and the port. The exception is the area around Plaza de Cairasco, which is heaving every evening as students gather outside the terrace bars of Old Stone's and the Hotel Madrid (► 66). Around the corner, Taberna de las Ranas is a popular night-time haunt on the edge of the Galería de Arte Monopol shopping centre. Across the road over in Vegueta, Quetal and Soul Train are cool bars for late drinks and music.

As the night wears on, **la movida** (the scene) shifts downtown. The bars on the north side of Plaza de España are lively around midnight, and there is plenty of action on the *terrazas* (terrace bars) around Parque Santa Catalina. The area between Parque Santa Catalina and the port is the seamier side of Las Palmas, and it is wise not to wander alone here at night. Most bars shut around 2am, but the discos stay open for a few hours after that.

The North

Getting Your Bearings

For many people, the north is the true essence of Gran Canaria. Las Palmas may be more exciting, the central mountains more dramatic, and the south more sunshine, but the real Gran Canaria is found in the fertile hills and valleys of the north. This is where the Guanche kingdoms established their capitals, at Telde and Gáldar. And, apart from Las Palmas, this is still where the majority of Canarios live, in towns like Arucas and Agaete, Gáldar and Guía, Telde and Teror, where tourism is important but where there is still more than one way of making a living.

The north is not without tourist ambitions, but the clouds which produce its famously green landscape are the same ones that keep most tourists away. When the trade winds reach Gran Canaria, they bring with them a thick bank of cloud that hovers over the north of the island and fills the air with moisture. Rain is not uncommon here, and sometimes

Punta de Ortiz

Punta de Sardina

434m
Pico de
Gáldar

Cenob
Valeró **4**

Sardina 12

Gáldar 11

GC2

Barrial

San Isidro

GC2

10

**Santa María
de Guía** GC700

Casa Muse

Punta de Cardonal

Puerto de
las Nieves

Agaete

837m
Viento

Tomás Morales

Moy

5 Valle de Agaete

GC200

San Pedro

GC75

Los Berrazales

1222m
Montaña
Buenaventura

GC70

Valles

GC21

GC21

Artenara

1773m
Mariscos

GC210

Cr
Tej

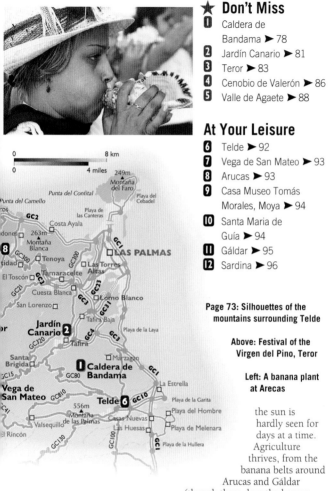

Page 73: Silhouettes of the mountains surrounding Telde

Above: Festival of the Virgen del Pino, Teror

Left: A banana plant at Arecas

the sun is hardly seen for days at a time. Agriculture thrives, from the banana belts around Arucas and Gáldar (though these days the banana industry is in serious decline) to the plains of San Mateo and the tropical valley of Agaete. Most of the fruit and vegetables which you can buy in Gran Canaria are grown in this area.

It is not just farming and fishing which have survived. Many of Gran Canaria's indigenous crafts are still produced here, from the pottery workshops of La Atalaya to the stonework of Arucas. This is also where you will encounter the most authentic town and village fiestas, such as the annual pilgrimage to Teror or the surviving pagan ritual of beating branches in the water in an effort to bring rain at Puerto de las Nieves.

You cannot claim to know Gran Canaria until you have spent some time in the north. There are some remarkable sights here, including a well-preserved Guanche granary and the island's most spectacular crater, but what most people remember are the small towns and villages, the markets and the volcanic hills which give this region its special character.

In Three Days

If you're not quite sure where to begin your travels, this itinerary
recommends a practical and enjoyable three-day tour of Northern
Gran Canaria, taking in some of the best places to see using
the Getting Your Bearings map on the previous page. For more
information see the main entries.

Day One

Morning
Spend the morning at the **2** **Jardín
Canario** (➤ 81, right), admiring its
collection of native Canarian plants
(right), then have a traditional
Canarian lunch at the restaurant
that overlooks the gardens.

Afternoon
A short drive leads to **1** **Caldera de
Bandama** (➤ 78), where you can
walk off your lunch with a hike
down into the crater or enjoy a
round of golf at Spain's oldest golf
club (below) before spending the
night at the **Hotel Golf Bandama**
(➤ 97).

Day Two

Morning
The road from Bandama to Santa
Brígida passes through **La Atalaya**
(➤ 79), where it is worth a brief
stop to see the Guanche-style
pottery, made at workshops. At
Santa Brígida, take the GC15
into the mountains, climbing
through pinewoods to **7** **Vega
de San Mateo** (➤ 93). At San
Mateo turn right towards **3** **Teror**
(➤ 83). After a twisting drive you
arrive in this town where you can
visit the basilica and museum.
Grill Lo Nuestro (➤ 98) is a good
place for lunch.

Afternoon
A minor road from Teror leads
to **8** **Arucas** (➤ 93), where you

can visit the neo-Gothic "cathedral" (right) and stroll through the streets and gardens of the town. Spend the night at **La Hacienda del Buen Suceso** (➤ 97), a smart rural hotel at the centre of a banana plantation.

Day Three

Morning

Drive down to the coast and take the GC2 towards **11 Gáldar** (➤ 95). When you reach the outskirts of Santa Maria de Guía, double back on the GC291 (the old road to Las Palmas) to visit the Guanche caves at **4 Cenobio de Valerón** (➤ 86). Afterwards, stop in **10 Santa Maria de Guía** (➤ 94) to taste the excellent local cheeses at Santiago Gil Romero's shop on the high street. Return to the GC2 and drive down to **Puerto de las Nieves** for a seafood lunch by the beach (➤ 98).

Afternoon

Take a walk around the harbour in Puerto de las Nieves, admiring the fishing boats and the **5 Dedo de Díos rock** (➤ 90, below). From here you can drive up the lush **5 Valle de Agaete** (➤ 88). If you feel like staying longer, the **Princesa Guayarmina spa hotel** (➤ 97) at the head of the valley offers peace, solitude, mountain walks and organic vegetables from their own farm.

❶ Caldera de Bandama

This perfectly formed crater (*caldera*), 1km (0.6 miles) wide and 200m (656 feet) deep, has walls of volcanic rock and a fertile valley at its centre. Although it has been dormant for hundreds of years, the existence of a "hot spot" just below the surface suggests that the volcano may yet erupt again. There are fine views over the crater from the nearby peak, and a walk down onto the valley floor gives a close-up look at Gran Canaria's volcanic scenery – not to mention its most isolated house.

The crater takes its name from Daniel Van Damm, a 16th-century Dutch farmer who first planted vines here. Begin by heading up to the **Pico de Bandama** (574m/1,883 feet) for the best overall view. A spiralling road leads up here from the village; from the bus stop it takes around 30 minutes to walk. The **views** from the peak stretch as far as Las Palmas and

Gran Canaria's *calderas* were formed millions of years ago

occasionally to Fuerteventura. The bowl-shaped crater is spread out beneath you, while across the crater the lush green fairways of Spain's oldest golf club (Real Club de Golf de Las Palmas) form a dramatic contrast to the dark volcanic ash below.

Entering the Crater

The **walk** down into the crater is straightforward enough but you need to be prepared for a steep, tiring climb on the way back. Allow at least 90 minutes, more if you have a bus to catch. The path begins by the bus stop. Follow the lane which runs downhill past a small group of houses and into the crater. The path is cobbled at first,

Borage growing in a field

but soon becomes slippery and you need good shoes. If you don't want to go the whole way, about halfway down there is a *mirador* built onto a rocky platform with excellent views.

From here the path drops down sharply to the crater floor, alive with olive trees, cactus, borage and broom. Just after passing a large boulder on your right, turn right and then immediately left on to a narrow path which makes a complete circuit of the valley. At the centre of the crater is a lone farmhouse, incongruously numbered 44. Two huge eucalyptus trees offer shade, and an old wine press is hidden

Fruit ripening on the tree

LA ATALAYA

The road from Bandama to Santa Brígida passes through La Atalaya, a village of cave houses whose inhabitants are famous for their unglazed pottery. Everything here is made in the aboriginal style, hand-shaped out of volcanic clay without the use of a wheel and baked in woodburners rather than electric kilns. The pottery is sold from cave workshops close to the village square, where murals of local potters pay tribute to this ancient art.

behind the shed. From the farmhouse, a path climbs back out of the crater. As you climb, look out for a group of **Guanche cave dwellings**, dramatically set into the crater walls.

The exposed strata of the *caldera*

TAKING A BREAK

The Hotel Golf Bandama (➤ 97) makes an excellent stop for lunch with superb views over the *caldera*. But for more choice and something less expensive head to Santa Brigida, noted for its excellent restaurants.

➕ 181 D2 ✉ 2km (1 mile) south of Tafira Alta, reached via GC110 from Las Palmas 🚌 311 from Las Palmas

CALDERA DE BANDAMA: INSIDE INFO

Top tips Take a **picnic** and **plenty of water** with you if you are walking down into the crater.
■ It is a good idea to wear long trousers for this walk because of the sharp bushes beside the narrow path.

In more depth It is possible to walk right **around the rim** of the *caldera*, with views down into the crater from every angle. This walk is around 3km (2 miles) long and takes 1.5 hours.
Start by taking the road from the village towards Pico de Bandama; after a few minutes, as the road bends to the left, look out for a small parking area to your right. From here a path leads to the ridge of the crater and continues around the rim. It is narrow in places and quite vertiginous, but experienced walkers will have no difficulty. After circling the crater, the path dips and then climbs to the edge of the golf-course, from where a short walk along the road leads back to the village.

② Jardín Canario

Despite their small size, the Canary Islands harbour an extraordinary abundance of plant life, with many varieties of cactus and wildflowers growing only here. The islands are a refuge for more than 500 endemic plant species and many of them can be seen close up at Spain's largest botanical garden.

Native Plants

These gardens were laid out in 1952 on the steep slopes of the Guiniguada ravine. Most visitors arrive at the upper entrance (buses from Las Palmas stop here), where there is a *mirador* and a bust of the historian and naturalist Don José de Viera y Clavijo. From here you can look out over the entire gardens and the network of paths snaking down into the gorge.

You could easily spend an hour or two exploring, but it is best to head for the lower entrance and work your way back up to the top. Begin in **Plaza Matías Vega**, dominated by Canary palms. Near here, the **Jardín de las Islas** contains native species including the cardón, a cactus-like shrub which grows on the hillsides and is the symbol of Gran Canaria.

Walk through the **Jardín de las Islas** to reach the Jardín de Cactus, with more than 2,000 varieties, including aloe vera and prickly pear, both prevalent on Gran Canaria. The path leads around the nursery to **Plaza Fernando Navarro**, where a small ornamental garden is devoted to the plants of Macronesia, the group of volcanic islands that includes the Canaries, Madeira and the Azores. Among the endemic species to be found here is the yellow-flowering Teror broom.

Cross the wooden bridge to return to the left bank and begin the climb out of the gorge. Passing through woods of

The cactus gardens include both native and imported species, such as these *echinocactus grusonii* from Mexico

Canary pine, you reach **Paseo de los Dragos**, a footpath lined with dragon trees. This distinctive tree, closely related to the yucca, is mostly found on Tenerife. Its bark can be scratched to produce a resin known as "dragon's blood" which was used by the original inhabitants of the Canary Islands as a medicine. The path climbs past a pair of twin dragon trees to return to the mirador.

Dragon trees were revered by the Guanches for their sacred and healing properties

TAKING A BREAK

The restaurant at the **upper entrance** to the gardens is known for its excellent Canarian cuisine.

🚩 181 D3 ✉ 7km (4 miles) from Las Palmas on GC110 to Tafira Alta
✉ 928/219-580 🕐 Daily 9–6 🚌 301, 302, 303 (ask the driver to drop you at the gardens' top entrance) 💲 Free

JARDÍN CANARIO: INSIDE INFO

Top tips If you are driving, you can reach the lower entrance to the gardens by taking a right fork in Tafira Alta and following the minor road to Las Palmas. However, there is not much parking down here and you may be better off using the large car-park at the upper entrance.

■ If you are coming by bus, the trip can be combined with the Caldera de Bandama (► 78), though you need to make an early start to give yourself enough time. Several buses a day connect Las Palmas with Bandama, stopping outside the Jardín Canario.

Hidden gem Look out for La Fuente de los Sabios (Fountain of the Wise), an unexpected man-made monument in a garden full of natural beauty. The fountain is dedicated to foreign naturalists who have worked in the Canaries – among them Sabin Barthelot and Philip Barker Webb, authors of the first natural history of the Canary Islands in 1835.

3 Teror

This charming town of cobbled streets, whitewashed houses and Spanish colonial architecture is also the centre of popular religion on Gran Canaria. Thoroughly restored and declared a historical monument in 1979, it is now a showpiece town where visitors come for a glimpse of Gran Canaria as it was.

Most people only stay for half an hour or so, which is a pity as Teror rewards a much longer visit. This is a place for ambling up and down side streets, or sitting in shady squares admiring the beautifully preserved stone mansions. Even a simple stroll along the main street, from the bus station to the basilica, turns into a voyage of discovery as your eyes are drawn constantly upwards by the details on the carved wooden balconies which adorn every façade.

The main street comes to an end at a large open square in front of the **Basílica de Nuestra Señora del Pino**. The Church of Our Lady of the Pine takes its name from an apparition of the Virgin rumoured to have appeared in a pine tree shortly after the Spanish Conquest of 1478. The statue of the Virgin dates from the 15th century and is revered across the island. Every year on 8 September, the anniversary of the original apparition, people make the pilgrimage from all over Gran Canaria for the island's biggest religious celebration.

The main street in Teror is lined with fine old Canario houses

The Virgin of the Pine is not only the patron saint of Gran Canaria, such is her status that she has also been awarded the honorary rank of captain-general in the Spanish army.

The **basilica** itself is a neo-classical structure, completed in 1767 but incorporating an octagonal tower from an earlier church on this site. The three aisles are divided by tall stone columns which rise to a coffered wooden ceiling. Above the altar, the Virgin sits beneath a silver canopy in her finely embroidered robes. The emeralds which once adorned the statue were stolen in an audacious robbery in 1975.

The complex of historic buildings behind the basilica includes the former episcopal palace. In the square in front of the church, the **Casa Museo de los Patrones de la Virgen del Pino** is one of the best surviving examples of a traditional Canarian town house. The house belongs to the Manrique de Lara family, custodians of the Virgin of the Pine, and has been in the same family since it was built in the 17th century.

The rooms, filled with family heirlooms, portraits and antique furniture, lead off from a central courtyard overlooked by a rickety wooden balcony.

A tour of the house gives a fascinating insight into the lives of the Canarian nobility. Don Agustín, who was born in 1909, still lives in the house during the fiesta of La Virgen del Pino (➤ 100).

Catch a glimpse of the courtyard of the Manrique de Lara family home

AY TEROR!
Ay Teror! is the title of a popular Canario folk song, with words by local historian Néstor Alamo (1906–94). The song can often be heard at festivals and is also featured on CDs by folklore groups such as Los Gofiones and Mestisay.

The town is renowned for its crafts, in particular basketwork, woodcarving, embroidery, textiles and crochet. You can see these at the Sunday market or in several shops in the town.

TAKING A BREAK

There are several cafés on and around Plaza del Pino. For a meal with a superb view, head down the road to Valleseco to the restaurant **Balcón de la Zamora** (➤ 98).

✚ 180 B3
🚌 216 from Las Palmas

Basilica
✉ Plaza del Pino
🕐 Mon 1–8, Tue–Fri 9–1, 3–8:30, Sat 9–8:30, Sun 7:30–7:30 💷 Free

Casa Museo de los Patrones de la Virgen del Pino
✉ Plaza del Pino ☎ 928/630-239 🕐 Mon–Fri 11–6, Sun 10–2 💷 Inexpensive

TEROR: INSIDE INFO

Top tip Visit Teror on a **Sunday morning**, when the area around the basilica is taken over by a lively **market**, with stalls selling breads, cheeses and the local speciality, a soft pâté-like version of spicy chorizo sausage.

Hidden gem Don't miss **Plaza Teresa de Bolívar** (below), a small square just off Plaza del Pino, named after the first wife of the revolutionary Simon Bolívar. This peaceful square features intricately carved stone benches and a Gothic fountain at its centre, as well as a bust of Bolívar, who is best known for liberating the South American colonies from Spanish rule. Teresa de Bolívar, who grew up in Teror, was the daughter of a noble Canario family. She died of yellow fever less than a year after her marriage to Simon Bolívar in 1801.

4 Cenobio de Valerón

This complex of honeycomb caves set into a natural arch in the rockface is not only the best-preserved but also the most accessible of all Gran Canaria's Guanche sites. Dating from before the time of the 15th-century Spanish invasion, these artificial caves are among the best examples of aboriginal rock-carving on the island.

The word *cenobio* means convent and it was once thought that this was a Guanche nunnery, housing *harimaguadas* (vestal virgins) and daughters of the nobility who were sent here in preparation for marriage and childbirth. Such places did exist, but these days archaeologists agree that the purpose of Cenobio de Valerón was in fact as a grain store.

Some 300 **chambers** are carved into the rock, linked by a network of steps and passages. Such granaries were built in high places to protect

SUMMIT MEETINGS
The summit above the caves, Montaña del Gallego, was a tagoror, a place of assembly where the Guanche council would meet with the guanarteme (king).

Right: The granary was protected by its hillside position

Below: The caves were originally built to store surplus grain after the harvest

them from attack, and volcanic rock was chosen as it was easily manoeuvred using tools made of stone and bones. This particular site was ideal. The natural overhang of the rock provided shelter from the rain, while its east-facing position ensured plentiful sun.

The caves are now open to the elements, but at one time they would have been covered by wooden doors in order to preserve the grain. Recent studies suggest that the various silos belonged to different families, identified by *pintaderas* (terracotta seals), whose designs were painted onto the walls. If this is true, it would indicate a high degree of social organisation among the pre-Hispanic people of Gran Canaria.

Access to the caves is by a steep staircase built into the rock. For reasons of safety and conservation, it is essential to stick to the path.

➕ 179 E4 ✉ 3km (2 miles) east of Guía on the old (GC 291) road to Las Palmas ☎ 618/607-896; www.cenobiodevaleron.com ⏰ Wed–Sun 10–5 🚌 103, 105 from Las Palmas 💶 Inexpensive

CENOBIO DE VALERÓN: INSIDE INFO

Top tip After two years of improvements you can now enter the complex on your own or on a guided tour.

5 Valle de Agaete

Arriving in Valle de Agaete from one of the south coast resorts feels like stepping onto another planet. This bucolic valley, with its startling array of colours and unique subtropical climate, forms such a contrast to the arid landscapes of the south that you have to pinch yourself to remember that you are still in Gran Canaria.

Until recently the northwest coast was considered remote, but a new motorway and fast ferry service have turned this area into a stepping-stone between Las Palmas and Tenerife. Development has followed, especially by the port, though the Agaete has retained much of its authenticity and charm.

The white-washed houses of Agaete in the heart of an agricultural district

Rural charm

The town of **Agaete** was founded in 1481; a plaque near the church records the greetings of King Juan Carlos on its 500th anniversary, recalling his visit to "this pretty corner of Spain". It is a peaceful and attractive spot, with picturesque whitewashed houses and wooden balconies overflowing with plants. Locals sit around outside the 19th-century church in the shade of Plaza de la Constitución, or stroll in the Huerto de las Flores, a botanical garden where Tomás Morales (➤ 94) found inspiration.

The 7km (4-mile) **Valle de Agaete** climbs gently from Agaete towards the pinewoods of the Tamadaba massif. This is a place of almost mythical beauty, scented with honeysuckle, jasmine, bougainvillea, geraniums and Canarian pine. The fertile slopes support mangoes, papaya, oranges,

Fruit and vegetables grow in the valley

The Ermita de la Virgen de las Nieves

lemons, grapefruit, avocados and figs. The road ends at **Los Berrazales**, where there is a spa hotel and a footpath leading to the high sierra. There are breathtaking views out to sea.

Puerto de la Nieves

Back in Agaete, an arched bridge leads across the mouth of the barranco to this one-time fishing port. It is said to have taken its name from the snow (*nieve*) which is often visible on Mount Teide on Tenerife. A small chapel, **Ermita de la Virgen de las Nieves**, is dedicated to the Virgin of the Snows, patron of local fishermen. Models of fishing boats hang from the wooden rafters, but the real treasure is a 16th-century Flemish triptych of the Virgin and Child by Joos Van Cleve. Only the central panel usually hangs here; the side panels, featuring St Antony and St Francis, are in the parish church at Agaete. The chapel is usually locked, though it is open for Mass on Saturday evening and Sunday morning.

Quiet during the week, Puerto de las Nieves gets crowded at weekends. There is a pebble beach in the inner harbour, for swimming and snorkelling, and seafood restaurants on the promenade. Up to eight ferries a day leave for Tenerife, an hour away by boat. From the harbour end of the beach you can look out over **Dedo de Díos** (Finger of God), a slender basalt pillar said to resemble a finger pointing to the heavens. It is silhouetted against the base of the cliffs at the start of the **Andén Verde** route.

A hotel in Puerto de las Nieves has been built close to an old Guanche cemetery. All that remains is a model of what the cemetery might have looked like. Among the finds was an 8th-century coffin, now in the Museo Canario in Las Palmas (➤ 52).

ANDÉN VERDE

The most spectacular coastal drive on Gran Canaria reaches its climax at the so-called Andén Verde (green platform), just north of San Nicolás de Tolentino. The best viewpoint is from the Mirador del Balcón, where there is space to pull off the road and walk down to the viewing platform beneath the car park. From here you look out along a rocky coastline to the headland of Punta Góngora. Bring some binoculars and you may be able to see dolphins basking out at sea. This drive can be incorporated into a complete circuit of the island (➤ 164).

TAKING A BREAK

The Dedo de Díos (Finger of God) provides a dramatic local landmark

Casa Romántica (➤ 98) is a popular restaurant with its own tropical gardens where bananas, citrus fruit and avocados are grown. Canaries sing and parrots squawk as you stroll around the grounds. If you don't want a full meal, go to the bar for a glass of fresh papaya juice or a cup of coffee from beans grown on the estate.

➕ 179 D3 🚌 103 from Las Palmas to Agaete and Puerto de las Nieves; 102 from Gáldar to Valle de Agaete

At Your Leisure

6 Telde

Gran Canaria's second town is almost totally off the tourist trail, yet it is easy to reach and has a very attractive and well-restored old quarter.

The most appealing area (*barrio*) is San Juan, reached by following the signposts from the large roundabout near the bus station. This was the site of the original Spanish settlement and it contains a number of Canario houses built in distinctive Mudéjar (Moorish-Gothic) style soon after the Spanish Conquest in 1478. The district is centred around a charming main square, Plaza San Juan, where the church of San Juan Bautista (open daily 9–12:30, 5–8) features an ornate

Wooden balconies painted in two shades of green in Telde

CUATRO PUERTAS

Telde was the capital of one of the two Guanche kingdoms on Gran Canaria and there are several archaeological sites around the town. The most important is Cuatro Puertas, 4km (2.5 miles) out of Telde on the road to Ingenio, where four separate entrances lead to a cave chamber where sacred rituals and fertility rites are believed to have been held.

Flemish altarpiece and a revered statue of Christ, sculpted out of maize (corn) by Mexican Indians in the 16th century. Behind the church, a small park contains a children's playground, caged birds and a miniature zoo.

Opposite the plaza, a narrow lane leads across an aqueduct past citrus trees to another historic barrio, San Francisco, with whitewashed houses, cobbled streets and an 18th-century church. The two districts are joined by Calle León y Castillo, named after the brothers Fernando (1842–1918) and Juan León y Castillo (1834–1912), the former a diplomat and politician, the latter the engineer responsible for Maspalomas lighthouse and Puerto de la Luz

in Las Palmas. Their **family home** is now a museum, with galleries displaying medals and 19th-century paintings. If you want to relax, Parque San Juan has footpaths and cycle trails, an open-air auditorium, botanical gardens and a lake.

🔲 181 E2 ⊠ Tourist information office, Calle León y Castillo 2 ☎ 828/013-331 🚌 12 from Las Palmas, 6 and 90 from Maspalomas

Casa Museo León y Castillo
⊠ Calle León y Castillo 43 ☎ 928/696-653 🕐 Mon–Fri 8–8, Sat 10–8, Sun & public hols 10–1 💲 Free

❼ Vega de San Mateo

This prosperous agricultural town at the foot of the sierra is best known for its weekly market, which begins on Saturday and reaches a climax on Sunday morning. Most of the action takes place in a large hangar on the edge of town, with stalls devoted to fruit, vegetables, olives, bread, eggs, cheeses and wine, as well as fresh flowers and dried herbs. There is also an open-air market featuring local crafts such as pottery and basketwork.

🔲 180 B2 🚌 303 from Las Palmas

❽ Arucas

This former banana town, now more or less a satellite of Las Palmas, is

A bottle of rum, produced in the main Arucas distillery

dominated by the extraordinary cathedral-like church of San Juan Bautista. Designed by the Catalan architect Manuel Vega March in neo-Gothic, Modernist style, it was built between 1909 and 1977 out of the local blue-grey stone. Although the church is modern, it contains a number of old works of art, including a Virgin and Child by Cristóbal Hernández de Quintana (1659–1725). By the altar is a beautiful sculpture of Christ, carved in wood in 1940 by local artist Manolo Ramos González.

The streets around the church contain several more buildings in the same volcanic stone, known as *piedra de Arucas* or *piedra azul* (blue stone). Most of them date from the late 19th or early 20th centuries. Look out for the Heredad de Aguas (the water consortium), a splendid neo-classical building opposite the gardens.

Arucas is the centre of rum production on Gran Canaria and on a tour of the **Arehucas distillery** you can see barrels signed by King Juan Carlos, Julio Iglesias, Tom Jones and Montserrat Caballé. Included are free tasting of rum and liqueurs.

FOR KIDS
The north of the island can be a bit lacking in the traditional things that keep children amused but there are things they might find enjoyable. Near Agaete, the secluded cove of El Juncal has exceptionally calm waters and is ideal for a family day out. Teenagers will prefer the bigger waves along the north coast that provide good surfing opportunities (► 100). A riding lesson at the Picadero de Real Club Las Pamas (► 100) can be fun, or why not take a ferry from Puerto del las Nieves across to Tenerife for the day?

Before you leave Arucas, drive up to the summit of **La Montaña**, the volcanic cone overlooking the town. The views stretch to Las Palmas and down to the north coast, with banana plantations visible all around. Bananas are still an important crop, but widespread competition from Africa and Central America means that the industry is in decline and these days much of the fruit is left to rot on the trees.

➕ 180 C4 ✉ Tourist information office, Plaza de la Constitución 2 ☎ 928/623-136
🕓 Church: Daily 9:30–12:30, 4:30–7:15
🚌 205, 210 from Las Palmas

Arehucas distillery
➕ 180 C4 ✉ Era de San Pedro 2 (2km/ 1 mile on the road to Gáldar) ☎ 928/624-900
🕓 Mon–Fri 10–2 💰 Free

❾ Casa Museo Tomás Morales

The poet Tomás Morales (1884– 1921) is known for his lyrical descriptions of his Gran Canarian homeland, and his birthplace in Moya has been turned into a small museum.

The charming old house has a peaceful garden and rooms full of antique furniture, manuscripts and first editions of Morales' books. There are examples of his poetry all over the walls.

Across the street, the parish church is precariously perched on the edge of a ravine, where two earlier churches fell into the gorge.

➕ 180 A4 ✉ Plaza de Tomás Morales, Moya
☎ 928/620-217 🕓 Daily 9–8
🚌 116, 117 from Las Palmas; 123 from Arucas
💰 Free

❿ Santa Maria de Guía

Steep cobbled streets fan out from a leafy main square in one of the oldest towns on Gran Canaria, founded in 1483 when the conquistador Pedro de Vera distributed land among his soldiers and local noblemen.

The religious artist and sculptor Luján Pérez (1756–1815), whose works crop up all over Gran Canaria, was born here. It was Pérez who designed the neo-classical façade of

A fountain plays in the square in front of the Church of Santiago de los Caballeros in Gáldar

the church of Santa María and there are several of his statues inside the church. The clock on the church tower was a gift from Pérez to the people of Guía.

However, the main reason for visiting Guía is to see Santiago Gil Romero (➤ 99), whose wonderfully old-fashioned cheese shop is the best place to buy *queso de flor*.

➕ 179 E4 🚌 103, 105 from Las Palmas

🔟 Gáldar

Gáldar was one of the two capitals of the Guanches on Gran Canaria and the town makes much of its historic role as the court of the *guanartemes* (Guanche kings).

Street names recall the town's pre-Hispanic past, and a statue in the town centre, unveiled by King Juan Carlos in 1986, pays homage to Tenesor Semidan, the last king of Gáldar, who was baptised by the Spanish monarchs and subsequently converted his people to Christianity.

Galdar's main attraction is the **Cueva Pintada** and the new museum and archaeological park. Although you cannot go in the cave, you can view the paintings through protective glass in the museum.

The most appealing part of the town is around Plaza de Santiago, a quiet square shaded by laurel trees in the shadow of a neo-classical church, built on the site of the palace of the Guanche kings.

Don't miss the enormous dragon tree in the courtyard of the town hall, which was planted in 1718.

✚ 179 E4 🚌 103, 105 from Las Palmas

Cueva Pintada
✉ Audiencia 2 ☎ 928/895-489; www.
cuevapintada.org 🕐 Tue–Sat 9:30–8 (last
visit at 6). Guided tours available 💵 Moderate

THREE GOOD MARKETS
- Arucas (Sat)
- Teror (Sun)
- Vega de San Mateo (Sat and Sun)

🗓 Sardina

Brightly painted fishing boats bob in the harbour at this cheerful fishing port in the far northwest corner of the island. During pre-Hispanic times this may have been a significant port, and there are still several cave dwellings, now used as boathouses and seafood restaurants. There are two dark-sand beaches, and you can swim off the rocks with views across the harbour to the wild west coast. More popular with locals than with tourists, this is a good place for a relaxing afternoon by the sea.

✚ 179 D4 🚌 103, 105 from Las Palmas to Gáldar (then 5km/3 miles to Sardina – take a taxi as there is no bus)

FIRGAS

The smallest town in Gran Canaria is famous for its mineral water. At the heart of the town is the much-photographed Paseo de Gran Canaria, a long flight of steps with a waterfall at the centre and a series of brightly coloured ceramic benches to one side (below). Each of the benches is devoted to one of the island's 21 municipalities, with a coat of arms and paintings of local scenes. Further up, Paseo de Canarias does the same thing for the seven Canary Islands. To get there, take bus Nos 201 or 202 from Las Palmas, or 202 or 211 from Arucas.

Where to... Stay

Prices

The symbols refer to the average cost of a double room in high season, generally November to April. All prices exclude 4.5 per cent sales tax (IGIC).

€ under €70   €€ €70–€130   €€€ over €130

ARUCAS

La Hacienda del Buen Suceso €€

This smart, rural hotel is set in a manor house on a large banana plantation. With only 18 rooms it never feels crowded and there is always space around the pool. Horse-riding and mountain bikes are available, and guests can wander around the estate. Come to be pampered; there's a Jacuzzi, fitness centre and Turkish bath.

+ 180 C4 ⊠ **Carretera de Arucas a Bañaderos, km1** ☎ **928/622-945; www.haciendabuensuceso.com**

CALDERA DE BANDAMA

Hotel Golf Bandama €€

The hotel beside the Royal Golf Club of Las Palmas (founded 1891), overlooks the crater of Bandama on one side and the golf-course on the other. Besides golf, other options include tennis, horse-riding and swimming. Excellent restaurant.

+ 181 D2 ⊠ **Caldera de Bandama** ☎ **928/351-538**

GÁLDAR

Hacienda de Anzo €€

This luxurious country house is decorated in a blend of Spanish colonial and Canarian style. The hotel is in a rural area but within a few kilometres of the coast to ensure a blend of country surroundings and trips to the beach. It is also in easy reach of the main road to Las Palmas, only 25km (15 miles) away. There are plenty of activities, with horse-riding and good hiking nearby but time too for relaxing by the pool and to appreciate the countryside.

+ 179 E4 ⊠ **Valle de Anzo, Gáldar** ☎ **928/551-655**

PUERTO DE LAS NIEVES

Puerto de las Nieves €€

This luxury hotel and hydrotherapy centre opened in 2000. Guests have free access to the spa pool and sauna, while optional extras include massage, reflexology and facials and a range of specialist anti-stress treatments. Most of the 30 rooms have a sea-facing terrace, and the beach is a couple of minutes away. The restaurant features Spanish and Canarian cuisine based on produce from the Valle de Agaete.

+ 178 C4 ⊠ **Avenida Alcalde José de Armas** ☎ **928/886-256**

VALLE DE AGAETE

Princesa Guayarmina €

The spa hotel at the head of the valley offers a range of treatments. Its restaurant features traditional Canarian cooking as well as vegetarian meals using produce from the hotel farm. A real get-away-from-it-all destination for a healthy holiday, with walks in the mountains and views out to sea. There is also a small outdoor pool.

+ 179 D3 ⊠ **Los Berrazales** ☎ **928/898-009**

Where to...
Eat and Drink

Prices

Expect to pay per person for a meal, excluding drinks and service

€ under €15	€€ €15–€30	€€€ over €30

Most restaurants on Gran Canaria are open throughout the year, though they may close at some time during the year for an annual holiday.

TEROR

Grill Lo Nuestro €

This friendly grillhouse is devoted to fresh local meat barbecued over an open fire. Wooden tables and benches complete the typical Canarian rustic look. You can also sample local cheese and snails, and *papas arrugadas* (▶ 23; served with *mojo* sauce) accompanied by a good house wine.

🔠 180 B3 ☒ Plaza de las Nieves el Palmar ☎ 928/631-229 ◎ Tue–Sun noon–5, 8–1. Closed Sep

Balcón de la Zamora €€

This restaurant does a brisk trade with coach tour parties who flock here for the fine views as well as for the excellent kid stew. As it isn't easily accessed by public transport, you will really need a car to get here independently.

🔠 180 B3 ☒ Carretera a Valleseco km 8 ☎ 928/618-042 ◎ Sat–Thu noon–11

VALLE DE AGAETE

Casa Romántica €€

Halfway up the Valle de Agaete, this restaurant is much frequented by tour groups who stroll in its gardens admiring the astonishing range of fruit trees and tropical plants. Although it mostly serves standard international cuisine, the restaurant also makes full use of the produce of its gardens, notably in the tropical fruit sorbets.

Another speciality is coffee, from the only coffee beans to grow in Gran Canaria. A shop sells packs of coffee for visitors to take home, as well as local produce such as aloe vera and papaya jam.

🔠 179 D3 ☒ Valle de Agaete ☎ 928/898-084 ◎ Daily 10–6

PUERTO DE LAS NIEVES

Las Nasas €€

The best of Canarian fish cooking is served at this simple beachside restaurant. The nautical theme dominates inside, with fishing nets, model boats and blue-and-white checked tablecloths, or you can eat out of doors on the terrace just a few steps from the beach, watching the sunbathers, fishing boats and ferries leaving for Tenerife.

Metal trays of red and green *mojo* sauce are brought by friendly waiters to your table, and the waiter will also recommend the fresh fish of the day, which you can have fried or grilled – though there are plenty of more elaborate seafood choices as well.

🔠 178 C4 ☒ Calle Nuestra Señora de las Nieves 6 ☎ 928/898-650 ◎ Daily noon–8

ARUCAS

Meson de la Montaña €€

This restaurant on the top of the volcano overlooking Arucas has a strong element of kitsch. Service is formal, with waiters in waistcoats and bow ties, and the menu includes Canarian and regional Spanish specialities, as well as unusual dishes such as beef in mango sauce. The extensive wine cellar includes Canarian bottles. Although the food is very acceptable, the main reason for coming here is the superb view, which takes in Las Palmas, the banana plantations and sometimes Tenerife. There is also a popular children's playground.

➕ 180 B2 ☒ Montaña de Arucas
☎ 928/600-844 🕐 Daily noon–midnight

SARDINA

Terraza del Ancla €€

This fish restaurant on the promenade captures the rustic atmosphere of the *chiringuitos*, those beach huts which used to be in all of Spain's fishing ports serving fried sardines caught freshly that day. You eat at plastic tables on the pavement, but the views and the colourful fishing boats make up for any discomfort. Ask the waiter for the fresh catch of the day, which

comes grilled, with toasted garlic and herbs. Paella and *sancocho* (Canarian fish stew) are served only at weekends. An experience to be thoroughly recommended – simple but delicious.

➕ 179 D4 ☒ Avenida Antonio Rosas
☎ 928/551-496 🕐 Daily noon–2am

SANTA BRIGÍDA

Restaurant Satautey €€–€€€

Sample accomplished cooking at the Hotel Escuela's smart restaurant (a working hotel and training school). French windows provide fine garden views while you tuck into the Canarian cuisine from the school's students, which wins plaudits. Dishes such as avocado *bavaroise* with pistachio oil and caviar are followed by fish battered in coconut, and to finish try the extraordinary roasted maize (*gofio*) ice cream, are all beautifully presented.

➕ 181 D3 ☒ Hotel Escuela Santa Brígida, Calle Real de Coello 2 ☎ 828/010-400
🕐 Mon–Sat 1:30–4, 8:30–11, Sun 1:30–4

Where to...
Shop

The weekly markets at Arucas (Saturday), Teror (Sunday) and Vega de San Mateo (Saturday, Sunday) have a good range of local produce, and there are daily covered markets at Arucas and Gáldar. The best place to buy pottery is in the cave village of La Atalaya (▶ 79).

ARUCAS

The Arehucas distillery shop (▶ 94) sells a range of light and dark rums along with rum-based liqueurs tasting of banana, orange, coffee, almonds or honey.

A small shop in **Plaza San Juan**, in front of the church, sells Guanche-style pottery and artefacts fashioned out of volcanic stone.

SANTA MARÍA DE GUÍA

Guía is famous for its *queso de flor* (literally "flower cheese"), made in the highlands from a mixture of cow's and sheep's milk and curdled with thistle flowers. The best place to buy it is from **Santiago Gil Romero** (Calle Marqués del Muni 34), on the main road running through the centre of town. The Romero family, in business for over 70 years, love their cheese and will share this love with anyone, proffering slices of mature *queso* and insisting that you wash it down with a glass of the local red wine. Cheeses mature on bamboo mats, the shelves are piled high with wine bottles, and wall posters tell the history of the product.

Where to...
Be Entertained

FESTIVALS

Fiesta del Queso deol Flor (late Apr/early May): lots of cheese-eating, traditional music and dancing at the home of cheese, Santa Maria del Guia.

San Juan Bautista (24 Jun): bonfires, dancing and cattle markets in Arucas and Telde in honour of their patron saint.

Santiago (25 Jul): traditional dancing and Canarian wrestling for the feast of St James in Galdar.

Bajada de la Rama (4 Aug): locals from Agaete collect pine branches from the mountains and carry them down to the sea, where they thrash the waves with them to pray for rain. This is one of the oldest festivals in Gran Canaria,

with rituals dating back to pre-Hispanic times.

Traida del Agua (12 Aug): locals shower visitors with water in the district of Lomo Magullo in Telde, in imitation of an ancient Guanche ritual whereby masses were offered to Alcorán, the god of rain.

Santa Maria de Guia (15 Aug): traditional celebrations in Guia in honour of the patron saint.

Fiesta de San Roque (16 Aug): the pretty town of Firgas celebrates its saint with fireworks, parades singing and dancing.

La Virgen del Pino (8 Sep): pilgrims converge on Teror from all over Gran Canaria, bringing carts laden with produce to lay at the feet of the Virgin in Gran Canaria's biggest popular religious festival.

Bajada del Cristo (Sep): the maize sculpture of Christ is taken down from the church in Telde and carried in procession through the streets of the town.

San Mateo (21 Sep): a pilgrimage and street parties in Vega de San Mateo held in honour of the patron saint.

Fiesta de la Manzana (first Sun in Oct): apple festival to celebrate the harvest in Valleseco, near Teror.

OUTDOOR ACTIVITIES

Golf

There are two golf courses in this region. A handicap certificate is advisable if you are thinking of visiting either of them. **Real Club de Golf de Las Palmas** (tel: 928/350-104) is the oldest golf club in Spain, founded in 1891 and situated on the edge of the Caldera de Banadama (▲ 78). The undulating course has narrow fairways and facilities include a driving range and a floodlit putting

green as well as a golf hotel. Visitors are welcome but you should try to avoid weekends. A second course opened in 2000 at **El Cortijo** near Telde (tel: 928/711-111), 6km (4 miles) south of Las Palmas on the GC1 motorway. El Cortijo also has an 18-hole pitch-and-putt course which is illuminated at night.

Horse-riding

Green ravines, spectacular cliffs and picturesque natural areas provide an ideal horse-riding landscape. Lessons and outings are available at the **Picadero de Real Club Las Palmas** (tel: 928/351-050).

Surfing

The waves along the **north coast** make for good surfing with bodyboards. Some of the best spots are the beaches of Bañaderos, Quintanilla and San Andrés near Arucas, San Felipe near Guia and Bocabarranco near Galdar. Surfing equipment and bodyboards can be hired at all of these beaches.

Central Mountains

Getting Your Bearings

Wild, windswept, majestic, magnificent, the centre of Gran Canaria is unique on the island. The mountains and valleys which make up the *cumbre* (central sierra) are the result of volcanic activity which began around 14 million years ago. Erosion has produced a stark, dramatic landscape of craters, gullies, canyons, cliffs and vast pillars of rock. Each new bend in the road reveals more startling views. The philosopher Miguel de Unamuno (1864–1937) called this area a "tempest of stone"; for the 17th-century historian Marín y Cubas, it was "a red ochre-coloured landscape like baked soil".

Two instantly identifiable landmarks stand guard over the skyline, following you around wherever you go. One is the vast bulk of Roque Bentaiga, a sacred place in earlier times and now the centre of an archaeological park. The other is Roque Nublo, tall and slender, whose familiar silhouette has become a symbol of Gran Canaria.

The red roofs and whitewashed houses of Artenara

Yet despite the grandeur of these impressive natural monuments, the mountains also have their softer side. There are villages of white houses surrounded by almond groves and palm trees, and in springtime the hillsides become a festival of colour, painted with wildflowers such as cistus, lavender and broom. The dense pinewoods which once

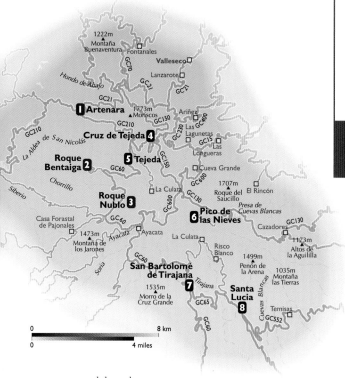

covered these slopes may
have disappeared, but the last
remaining forest of Canary pines at Tamadaba is a reminder of
what might have been.

There are two ways of exploring this region. Most people
visit the mountains on a day trip from the coast, dashing
through in a hire car and admiring the scenery through their
windscreen. If this is all you have time for, do it – it will be
one of the highlights of your trip. Alternatively, if you can,
stay the night, get out in the mountains, breathe the air, smell
the wild herbs, hike along the old mule paths and ancient
pilgrim routes that are being carefully restored, and you will
experience a side of Gran Canaria that few visitors ever see.

In Two Days

If you're not quite sure where to begin your travels, this itinerary
recommends a practical and enjoyable two-day tour of Central Gran
Canaria, taking in some of the best places to see using the Getting
Your Bearings map on the previous page. For more information see
the main entries.

Day One

Morning
Spend the morning in **1 Artenara**
(➤ 106), Gran Canaria's highest
town, enjoying views across the
sierra. Climb up to the cave
chapel above the town before
eating lunch in one of Artenara's
lovely restaurants.

Afternoon
Walk off lunch with a stroll in the Tamadaba pine woods. From the car-
park and picnic area, a wide track leads through the woods to a series of
reservoirs. Complete the circuit of the woods by car, enjoying the views of
Tenerife across the water. Return through Artenara and **5 Tejeda** (➤ 114;
church pictured above) to **4 Cruz de Tejeda** (➤ 113; below), where you can
stay the night at **El Refugio** (➤ 117). Alternatively, confident drivers can
make a scary, twisting and turning road which begins around 3km (2 miles) east o
Tamadaba. Although the distances are not great, you would probably need
the whole afternoon for this trip.

Evening
Climb the hill behind **El Refugio** after a good meal to watch the sun set.

Day Two

Morning

Follow the snaking road downhill back towards Tejeda, with the two monoliths of Roque Bentaiga and Roque Nublo looming large over the landscape. After bypassing Tejeda, take the right turn to **2 Roque Bentaiga** (➤ 108; above), where you can visit the information centre and climb the short path towards the rock. Continue south to Ayacata for lunch at one of the roadside bars. In the village have a coffee and try the local speciality *mazapan* (almond cake) or buy some to take home as a present.

Afternoon

Take the minor road from Ayacata to Cruz de Tejeda. A stone cross marks the centre of Gran Canaria at the top of the mountain pass. The first stop is La Goleta car park, the start of the path to **3 Roque Nublo** (➤ 110). After climbing to the summit, continue on this road, passing almond groves and campsites before reaching a crossroads. Turn right at the crossroads for **6 Pico de las Nieves** (➤ 114), Gran Canaria's highest peak. After taking in the views, return along the same road, stopping at the Mirador de Becerra to appreciate the view on the way (➤ 113).

❶ Artenara

At an altitude of 1,260m (4,134 feet), Artenara is the highest town on Gran Canaria, with unrivalled views over the central sierra and the pine-covered hills. It is also one of the oldest towns on the island, continuously inhabited since before the Spanish invasion of 1478. Artenara was the Guanche name for the town; it was changed by the Spanish conquerors to San Matías de Artenara, but has since reverted to its original name.

The earliest inhabitants carved cave dwellings out of the rock and many of these are still lived in today. Some of the caves have become second homes for the people of Las Palmas, and others are let out as holiday cottages. The best-known cave in Artenara is the sanctuary housing the **Virgen de la Cuevita** (Virgin of the Cave), the focus of one of the island's most spectacular festivals (➤ 32). The chapel is believed to have been built by 14th-century Mallorcan monks who visited Gran Canaria as missionaries before the Spanish Conquest and enlisted local converts to help.

To find the chapel, follow the signs to La Cuevita from the church square at the centre of town. Only the belfry on the roof suggests that there is anything special about this cave. The present **chapel** dates from the 17th century, with an altar, pulpit, choirstand and confessional hewn out of the red volcanic rock. Inside a niche sits the carved wooden statue of the Virgin, with the infant Christ in her arms.

The humility of this scene contrasts sharply with Artenara's other notable sight, a huge Rio de Janeiro-style **statue of Christ** with arms outstretched standing on a hilltop overlooking the town. It is worth climbing up here for the **views** of the *cumbre*. The two principal landmarks, Roque Bentaiga (➤ 108) and Roque Nublo (➤ 110), are clearly visible on the skyline and there is a vast panorama over the Tejeda valley and the surrounding cliffs. Beneath the statue of Christ, a tunnel leads through the mountain.

An enormous statue of Christ dominates the town

On the northern edge of Artenara, above the park, there is a *mirador* with a vista of the Tamadaba pinewoods. The **Pinar de Tamadaba** is the last surviving primeval forest on Gran Canaria and it is covered with Canary pines which grow to more than 30m (100 feet) high. A one-way circuit leads around the forest, where pine cones and needles are strewn across the road. There are many footpaths here, as well as a picnic area.

The cave village of **Lugarejos**, near Tamadaba, is a centre of production for traditional pottery. All the raw materials are

The view from Artenara

gathered locally – red ochre, clay, pine needles and cones, which fuel the kilns. The earthenware can be bought at an interpretation centre in Lugarejos (tel 928/666-117).

TAKING A BREAK

La Esquina (➤ 117) offers honest Canarian food and is worth a visit for the views alone.

➕ 179 E2 ✉ 220 from Las Palmas (limited timetable – three times a day)

ARTENARA: INSIDE INFO

Top tip Remember that it can get very **cold** up here in winter and even on summer evenings.

In more depth The flat-topped tableland at **Acusa**, near Artenara, was the site of a Guanche settlement and is one of only three places in Gran Canaria where mummies have been found. It lies at the start of a spectacular drive, with narrow roads tumbling down to the Barranco de la Aldea and returning through the village of **El Carrizal** (➤ 115). The mummies, which were wrapped in cured goalskins and placed in woven rush bags, are on display in the **Museo Canario** in Las Palmas (➤ 52).

② Roque Bentaiga

This 1,404m (4,606-foot) outcrop, left behind by volcanic eruptions more than 3 million years ago, was both a sacred area and a place of refuge for the Guanches. Recent excavations have uncovered several groups of cave houses, together with barns, cattle pens and burial sites. An *almogarén*, a place of ritual worship and sacrifice that the Guanches built in the highest and least accessible places on the island, was found here. Some of the caves are painted with fertility symbols, and this is also where the first discoveries of aboriginal writing using a version of the Libyan-Berber alphabet were made.

According to historical accounts, Roque Bentaiga was the site of a fierce **battle** in 1483 as the Spanish conquerors attempted to subdue the Canario natives. One of the conquerors, Sedeño, has described how the Canarios fled to Bentaiga following a defeat at Ajodar (La Aldea): "Short of provisions, the Canarios and their leader abandoned Ajodar at nightfall and started their climbing march along the San Nicolás valley on their way to another fortress known as Bentaiga, where they managed to obtain supplies. The stronghold is surrounded by cliffs at the top of which there are several caves with capacity for many people, although the paths leading up to them are dangerous."

It is easy to see how this isolated rock could provide a natural fortress. Chronicles of the conquest describe how

Roque Bentaiga stands out above the mountain landscape

ROQUE BENTAIGA: INSIDE INFO

In more depth Cueva del Rey, 2km (1 mile) west of Roque Bentaiga, is one of the largest man-made caves in Gran Canaria, approximately 20m (66 feet) long and 11m (36 feet) wide. The name suggests that it was used by a Guanche king (*rey*) but it seems to have been divided into a series of smaller chambers, which may have been used as sanctuaries or meeting places. The entrance to the cave can be seen high in the cliff face near a hamlet of shepherds' houses. Some of the nearby caves are still in use as sheep pens.

the Spaniards attempted to starve the Canarios out, only to be met by a hail of boulders which caused heavy casualties. Eventually a battle took place, with the Christians led by Pedro de Vera, assisted by Tenesor Semidan, the former king of Gáldar who had converted to the Spanish side with his followers. It was these Canarian "traitors" who saved the day for the Spanish. Although there were many deaths on both sides, the Guanches were defeated and forced to flee to their final stronghold at Fortaleza Grande near Santa Lucía (► 115).

All of this is explained at the small archaeological park's eco-museum beside Roque Bentaiga. The captions are in Spanish but there is a booklet available in English, with accounts of the historical and archaeological discoveries.

A **path** from the museum leads up towards the summit. The path is straightforward at first, but after a few minutes it runs out and the rest of the journey is rather a scramble.

TAKING A BREAK

For a substantial meal or snacks you will have to travel to the nearest town of Tejeda. Alternatively, take a picnic.

➕ 179 E1   ✉ 4km (2.5 miles) southwest of Tejeda

Archaeological park's museum
🕐 Daily 10–6   💲 Inexpensive

③ Roque Nublo

It may not quite be the highest point on the island, but Roque Nublo (Cloud Rock) is undoubtedly the most emblematic of Gran Canaria's peaks. Its distinctive, slender silhouette can be seen from right across the sierra and the short climb on to the plateau makes a popular weekend walk.

The tall basalt monolith stands on a ridge above the village of **Ayacata**. The easiest way of getting there is to leave your car in the small car park at La Goleta, on the minor road from Ayacata to Cruz de Tejeda. From here a wide trail heads towards the summit, passing the smaller figure of El Fraile (the friar), named after its resemblance to a praying monk.

There is a choice of paths to the **summit**, but the most direct route takes around 45 minutes each way. The climb is straightforward, but testing in places. Make sure you take plenty of water.

It begins with a **gentle ascent** through hillsides of euphorbia and broom, then grows steeper as you climb through the pinewoods beneath El Fraile. There are fine views over Ayacata, nestling in the valley to your left. After a succession of zigzags you come to a junction, where you could go straight ahead to make a complete circuit of the rocks. Instead, to reach the summit, take the higher path to your left. The path narrows as it ascends to a pass, where a rock-laid trail leads steeply to the plateau.

There are splendid **views** from here, with the white town of Agaete to the northwest, and Tenerife on the horizon; and to the northeast the three distinctive hills of La Isleta in Las

Roque Nublo rises above the town of Tejeda

The village of Tejeda sits in the shadow of Roque Nublo

Palmas. To the east, terraced hillsides lead down to the village of La Culata, while behind you El Fraile and the car park remind you how far you have climbed.

Up close, Roque Nublo appears much bigger than it does from a distance. It is actually 65m (213 feet) tall, and only serious climbers should attempt to scale the rock face.

For a **longer walk**, return to the pass beneath the plateau and turn right along a gravel path to make a complete circuit of the massif, enjoying views of Roque Nublo from every direction. The rule is simple – whenever there is a choice of paths, keep to the right. The path is easy, though there is plenty of vegetation so you may pick up a few scratches. The

DID YOU KNOW?

The white painted circle near the summit of Roque Nublo is said to mark the geographical centre of Gran Canaria.

undulating path winds its way past boulders and through thickets of borage, broom and pine, passing beneath the northern face of Roque Nublo, from where the rock appears to be balanced on its peak.

After around 30 minutes, a steep ascent leads back to the junction to rejoin the route to the car park.

The two monoliths at the summit are known as "father and son"

TAKING A BREAK
There are several roadside bars in nearby Ayacata.

 179 E1

ROQUE NUBLO: INSIDE INFO

Top tips Try to arrive **early** in the day – the sun is less intense, the views are better and there is more space in the tiny car park.

■ Even in summer it can be **cold and windy** at the summit, so take a sweater or a warm jacket.

■ To do this walk **without a car** you would need to take bus No 18 from San Fernando at 8am and walk up to Roque Nublo from Ayacata. The return bus leaves Ayacata at around 4:45pm. Make sure to check the bus times before you set out.

At Your Leisure

4 Cruz de Tejeda

A carved stone cross marks the notional centre of Gran Canaria at the top of this mountain pass (1,450m/4,757 feet).

Cruz de Tejeda has always been something of a crossroads – for pilgrims, shepherds and traders – and these days it has a new role as the commercial and tourist centre of the Central Mountains.

During the day, there is a bazaar-like atmosphere as coach parties descend on the square and the hawkers compete to offer donkey rides or sell souvenirs. In the evening, after the coach parties have left, there is a very different atmosphere and you can stroll among the Canary pines and chestnut trees enjoying the views or climb the path behind El Refugio Hotel (➤ 117) to watch the sun set over the sierra.

PICNIC AREAS

The environment agency has set up a number of roadside picnic areas in Gran Canaria. All of these are equipped with wooden tables and benches, and some have other facilities including barbecues, WCs, drinking water and children's playgrounds.

Among some of the most popular are:

Cueva de las Niñas (by the reservoir of the same name, southwest of Ayacata on the GC605)

Llanos de la Paz (on the road from Roque Nublo to Cruz de Tejeda)

Montaña de Santiago (between Ayacata and the Chira reservoir)

Pinar de Tamadaba (in the pine woods near Artenara)

In addition to the hotel, there is a *parador* designed in Canario style by Néstor Martín Fernández de la Torre in 1938. It has been closed for repairs for some time, and is expected to reopen to accommodate paying guests in 2009.

Cruz de Tejeda is at the centre of the network of *caminos reales* (royal roads), with footpaths leading to Artenara, San Mateo and Teror. A short walk leads to the Mirador de Becerra, for splendid views of the surrounding countryside.

🚹 179 F2 🚌 305 from Las Palmas (but very infrequent; best to go by car or in an organised tour)

A close-up view of the bell-tower on the Church of Our Lady in Tejeda

5 Tejeda

This quiet village of white houses at the head of the Barranco de Tejeda is overlooked by the vast Roque Bentaiga (➤ 108). The main street takes the form of a balcony, with a promenade giving views over the valley below. Most of the inhabitants live on the terraced slopes beneath the church square, where almonds and citrus fruits grow. In early springtime the fields are carpeted with almond blossom, making a splendid sight and a good excuse for the festival El Almendro en Flor, usually held in the first week of February (➤ 118).

🔢 178 C3 🚌 305 from San Mateo, 18 from Maspalomas

Sleepy San Bartolomé de Tirajana can be seen through the palm trees

6 Pico de las Nieves

At 1,949m (1,211 feet) above sea level, Pico de las Nieves (Snow Peak) is the highest point on Gran Canaria. The summit is used as a military base, but a lookout point just below the peak offers views over the sierra and the west of the island. Near the entrance to the military base is a recently restored well, Pozo de las Nieves, built by monks in 1699 in order to store the winter snows. The snow would be packed tightly beneath a layer of straw and when it turned to ice, it would be transferred to Las Palmas by mule for use in hospital operations in summer.

🔢 180 B1

7 San Bartolomé de Tirajana

It is sometimes hard to believe that this small rural township is

El Carrizal, on the slopes of a mountain is
reached by a narrow, winding road

the capital of the municipality that
controls the south coast resorts of
Maspalomas and Playa del Inglés.

Life goes on at a gentle pace,
and the biggest excitement is the
Sunday morning market, which
takes place in the square around
the 17th-century church. The same
square contains the town hall, with
wooden galleries and an attractive
inner courtyard. The nearby bars sell
guindilla, the local cherry brandy.

San Bartolomé stands at the head
of the Barranco de Tirajana on the
site of an earlier Guanche settlement
known as Tunte. This is believed to
have been a sacred site; when the
conquerors came, they brought with
them an image of St James, giving
rise to the popular name for the
town, Santiago de Tunte. From the
mirador (lookout point) to the south
of town there are views down the
barranco (gorge) all the way to the
south coast.

☐ 184 B4 ☐ 18 from Playa del Inglés/
Maspalomas, 34 from Agüimes

8 Santa Lucía

One of the prettiest villages on the
island has become a magnet for the
kind of rural tourism which Gran
Canaria is hoping to attract. As you

OFF THE BEATEN TRACK
The isolated village of El Carrizal
clings to the steep slopes of a gorge
above the Parralillo reservoir. The
village bar has a terrace with views
over the gorge and, if you're lucky,
and it's open, the owner will rustle
up something for you to eat in
the church square. Nothing much
grows here apart from palm trees
and prickly pear and it's difficult
to believe that anyone could live
somewhere so remote, especially on
a small island.

El Carrizal is reached by a snaking
drive on a narrow road which leaves
the GC60 around 3km (2 miles)
north of Ayacata. The road continues
down to the reservoir, where you can
turn right through a tunnel in the
rock for the long climb to Artenara.
To do this drive you need nerves of
steel and a good hire car. The road
is in good condition but is frequently
affected by rockfalls, and there are
few barriers in place to prevent you
from crashing into the ravine. Use
your horn on bends to warn other
drivers of your presence.

For an equally spectacular drive,
a left turn at the reservoir leads
through the Barranco de la Aldea
and down to the coast at San
Nicolás de Tolentino.

FILLING STATIONS
There are few filling stations in the mountains; most are located in the main towns such as Artenara and Tejeda, so fill up before you head inland

wander around the village you come across wooden signs for *casas rurales* (cottages for rent) and *caminos* (footpaths), making this a suitable base for a holiday in the mountains, yet within easy reach of the coast.

Tourists visit Santa Lucía, yet few of them get further than the Museo Castillo de la Fortaleza, a mock castle in the gardens of the Hao restaurant (➤ 117). The castle houses a museum of Canarian life, with exhibits ranging from Roman amphorae and Guanche pottery to old weapons, farming implements and stuffed birds. Take your time to explore the rest of the village, with

The lights of Santa Lucía glow in the gentle light at dusk, against a backdrop of mountains

palm trees, gardens and an imposing white-domed neo-classical church.

South of Santa Lucía, a trail leads to Fortaleza Grande, a fortress-like rock which was the Guanches' final stronghold following their defeat at Roque Bentaiga (➤ 108) in 1483. Ignoring the commands of their leader, Tenesor Semidan, to surrender to the Spanish conquerors, some of the 1,600 men and women, who had retreated to this place, threw themselves off the cliffs to their deaths.

➕ 184 B4 🚌 34 from Agüimes or San Bartolomé de Tirajana

Museo Castillo de la Fortaleza
✉ Calle Tomás Arroyo Cardosa ☎ 928/798-007 🕐 Daily 9–5 💶 Inexpensive

FOUR MOUNTAIN VILLAGES
■ Cercados de Araña
■ El Carrizal
■ La Culata
■ Las Lagunetas

Where to...
Stay

Prices

The symbols refer to the average cost of a double room in high season, generally November to April. All prices exclude 4.5 per cent sales tax (IGIC).
€ under €70 €€ €70–€130
€€€ over €130

CRUZ DE TEJEDA

El Refugio €€

There are only ten rooms in this alpine lodge, decorated in Canarian style but with all modern comforts. There is a small pool in the garden, and a cosy lounge. Climb the path behind the hotel for sunset biews.

🕇 179 F2 ◻ Cruz de Tejeda
☎ 928/666-513;
www.hotelruralelrefugio.com

Where to...
Eat and Drink

Prices

Expect to pay per person for a meal, excluding drinks and service
€ under €15 €€ €15–€30 €€€ over €30

Most restaurants on Gran Canaria open throughout the year, though they may close during the year for an annual holiday.

ARTENARA

La Esquina €€

This restaurant has fine views over the valley from its terrace. The cuisine is typically Canarian, the town being known for its grilled meat. A classic dish from Artenara is potaje de berros (watercress stew) and tortillas de calabaza (pumpkin pancakes) are also a local speciality.

🕇 179 E2 ◻ Artenara ☎ 928/666-631
🕔 Mon–Sat lunch only

CRUZ DE TEJEDA

Restaurante Centennial €€

Cruz de Tejeda is a very different place after dark, when the restaurant in this hotel is the only place to eat. Most of the diners are hotel guests filling up after a walk in the mountains. The food is typically Canarian.

🕇 179 F2 ◻ Hotel El Refugio, Cruz de Tejeda ☎ 928/666-188 🕔 Daily noon–3, 8–10

SANTA LUCÍA

Hao €€

Although this is popular with tourists, you will find it is still a good place to try authentic Canarian cuisine, seated at heavy wooden tables with sawn-off tree-trunks for stools. Grills are the speciality, along with marinated olives, papas arrugadas (➤ 23) and fresh goat's cheese.

🕇 184 B4 ◻ Calle Tomás Arroyo Cardosa
☎ 928/798-007 🕔 Daily 9–7

SAN BARTOLOMÉ DE TIRAJANA

La Hacienda del Molino €€

Opened in late 2006, this buzzing restaurant fronts a hotel occupying a restored hacienda. The the traditional Canarian food has gained a good reputation with the locals. There is also a working mill on the premises.

🕇 184 B4 ◻ Calle Los Naranjos 2
☎ 928/127-344; www.lahaciendadelmolino.com 🕔 Daily 1–4.30, 7–10

Where to...
Shop

There are few opportunities for shopping here, though T-shirts and souvenirs are sold from **roadside stalls** at Cruz de Tejeda. Other stalls feature local produce, almonds, almond cake, dried fruits and *bienmesabe* (almond syrup).

In Tejeda, **Dulcería Nublo**, a pastry shop, sells almond biscuits and *mazapan* (almond cake).

In Artenara you will find pottery, basketware and hand-woven cloth on sale. The town is actively promoting the revival of Canarian handicrafts.

Local traditional pottery is available in the cave craft village Lugarejos (▲ 106) and you will also find pottery and Canarian handicrafts in the mountain town of Santa Lucía (▲ 115).

Where to...
Be Entertained

FESTIVALS

El Almendro en Flor (early Feb): almond blossom festival takes place in Tejeda (▲ 114) with tastings of local produce.

San Isidro (15 May): agricultural fair in Artenara (▲ 106) with music, dancing and folklore performances.

Santiago de Tunte (25 Jul): pilgrimages and religious processions in San Bartolomé de Tirajana (▲ 114) take place in honour of the patron saint.

La Virgen de la Cuevita (last Sun in Aug): folk dancing, fireworks and a procession in Artenara (▲ 106).

La Virgen del Socorro (15 Sep): an image of the Virgin is taken

down from the church in Tejeda (▲ 114) and paraded around the town by participants.

Santa Lucía (13 Dec): this Swedish winter festival brings together Scandinavian and Canarian traditions and a week of street parties in honour of the patron saint of Santa Lucía (▲ 115).

Festival de los Labradores (20 Dec): in Santa Lucía people celebrate the workers' festival by dressing in peasant costume and carrying traditional farming tools.

OUTDOOR ACTIVITIES

Walking, cycling, fishing and hunting are all popular leisure activities in the Central Mountains, which offer stunning scenery.

The best **walking** is along the restored network of *caminos reales* (royal roads), footpaths and mule tracks which were once the main routes across the island. Walking maps and guides can be bought at the government bookshop in Las Palmas (▲ 70). **Free Motion** (▲ 150) offers guided mountain walks, including to Roque Nublo and Pico de las Nieves. Conditions in the mountains are more changeable than on the coast, and you will need extra clothing as well as food, water and sturdy shoes.

Fishing is possible in the reservoirs of Chira and Cueva de las Niñas, though you will need to obtain a licence. Ask where to get one at the nearest tourist office.

Spectator sports

The El Corte Inglés **rally-driving** event takes place over two days in April on a circuit which includes Ayacata, Artenara and Cruz de Tejeda, website: www.rallydecanarias.com

The South

Getting Your Bearings

The Gran Canaria of the holiday brochures begins in San Agustín and follows an arc around the south coast to Puerto de Mogán. This is a land of golden beaches and sunny skies. The trade winds and clouds that blow across the north of the island stack up in the Central Mountains, so the south coast basks in year-round sunshine. In winter you can be sunbathing on the beaches while snow is visible on the hills.

Despite the attractions of Las Palmas and the growth of inland tourism, the vast majority of visitors to Gran Canaria stay on the south coast. Many people arrive at the airport and head straight down to the coast for their holiday, finding that a single resort meets all of their needs. Each of the resorts has its own particular character – young or old, chic or cheerful, sporty or sedate. Puerto Rico appeals to families and watersports enthusiasts, San Agustín to older couples, and Playa del Inglés to the party-loving crowd. Maspalomas and Puerto de Mogán are fashionable and upmarket. In some places, tourism has undoubtedly scarred the landscape, but in others, such as the villas of Puerto de Mogán or the serried ranks of apartment blocks at Puerto Rico, it has contributed new and dramatic landscapes of its own.

You don't have to go far inland to experience a very different Gran Canaria. Peaceful towns and villages such as

Agüimes and Fataga, and monumental barrancos (gorges) that sweep down the mountains to the sea, are all just a short drive away. Even on the wild west coast beyond Puerto de Mogán, it is still possible to discover an isolated beach and a glimpse of Gran Canaria as it was.

Page 119: Puerto de Mogán at dusk

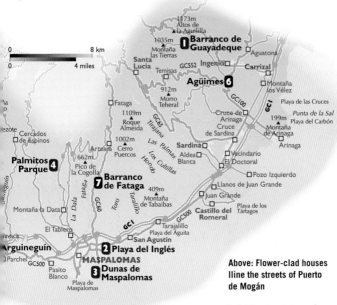

Above: Flower-clad houses lline the streets of Puerto de Mogán

Left: The church towers over the houses of Aguimes

In Two Days

If you're not quite sure where to begin your travels, this itinerary recommends a practical and enjoyable two-day tour of Southern Gran Canaria, taking in some of the best places to see using the Getting Your Bearings map on the previous page. For more information see the main entries.

Day One

Morning
Take the road from Agüimes into the ❶ Barranco de Guayadeque (➤ 124; below) to experience the natural splendour and unique character of this gorge. After coffee in the village of Cuevas Bermejas (➤ 126), continue to the end of the road for lunch at Tagoror (➤ 145).

Afternoon
Leaving the valley, take time for a brief stroll around the old quarter of ❻ Agüimes (➤ 138) before driving down to the coast at ❷ Playa del Inglés (➤ 127). The quickest and most direct route is on the GC1 motorway, but a more scenic alternative is the twisting mountain drive through Santa Lucía and the ❼ Barranco de Fataga (➤ 138). Arriving in Playa del Inglés, head straight down to the beach for a promenade along the Paseo Costa Canaria, followed by a sunset stroll across the ❸ Dunas de Maspalomas (➤ 130).

Evening
After dinner at a beachside restaurant, check out the action in the Kasbah and Yumbo centres (➤ 148), the two liveliest places to be at midnight and into the early morning.

Day Two

Morning
Allow yourself a couple of hours to wander around 4 Palmitos Parque (➤ 134), taking in the bird of prey and parrot shows (above) before a light lunch at the terrace café.

Afternoon
If you have children, take them to Aqualand (right, on the same road as Palmitos Parque, ➤ 134) to spend the afternoon enjoying the wave pools, waterslides and lazy river. Alternatively, take the old coast road through 8 Arguineguín (➤ 139) and spend an hour or two topping up your tan on the beach at 9 Puerto Rico (➤ 141).

Evening
Continue on the coast road to 5 Puerto de Mogán (➤ 136) for a drink beside the harbour while the sun sets behind the cliffs. After a walk around the marina, have your evening meal here, and enjoy the fresh local fish at Restaurante Cofradía (➤ 146).

❶ Barranco de Guayadeque

Not far from the crowded beaches of the south coast, there are people who still live in caves and tend their goats much as their ancestors must have done before the Spanish arrived. In this spectacular gorge between Agüimes and Ingenio, the spiritual descendants of the Guanches are doing their best to keep alive the pre-Hispanic lifestyle of Gran Canaria.

Natural landscape

The Barranco de Guayadeque slices across the landscape from the high mountains down to the coast. Its Guanche name means "a place of running water", and it was once a riverbed filled with reeds. It is still home to some 80 endemic species of **flora**, including a native variety of rock-rose, and Canary palms and euphorbia grow on the valley floor. The entire gorge has now been designated a nature reserve and archaeological park.

The road to Guayadeque follows the valley floor

Cave settlements

Many of the exhibits in the Museo Canario in Las Palmas
(➤ 52) were discovered in Guayadeque, and it is clear that
this was the site of a significant **Guanche settlement**. The
earliest inhabitants built cave houses on the sunny, eastern
side of the valley and burial caves for their dead on the shady
western side. As you enter the canyon, you can make out
some of the entrances to the caves high in the valley walls.
Most of them are inaccessible.

A paved road from Agüimes leads down to the valley floor,
soon reaching the village of **Cuevas Bermejas** (scarlet caves),
where several cave dwellings have been carved into a cliff face
of red volcanic rock. Opposite the car park, a path climbs the
hillside towards the cave houses, many of which have modern
amenities such as solar panels and TV aerials. Patios, pets and
window-boxes overflowing with plants complete the domestic
scene. Some of the villagers keep their cars in cave garages,
while others use the caves as shelters for goats and chickens,
climbing the hillside each day to the pastureland on the higher
plateau. Cave bars in the village serve snacks such as olives and
papas arrugadas (➤ 23), and there is a simple chapel hewn out
of the rock. The names of the gods may have changed and living
here may now be a lifestyle choice rather than a necessity, but
the people of Cuevas Bermejas are perhaps the closest living
relatives of the 15th-century aborigines of Gran Canaria.

Beyond Cuevas Bermejas, the walls rise to a height of 300m
(984 feet) and terraced fields of almonds begin to appear on
the slopes, carpeting the valley with a layer of white blossom
in spring. There is a roadside picnic area at **Montaña de las
Tierras**, with benches, tables and barbecues in the shade of
two eucalyptus trees. A little further on, the road runs out at
Tagoror (➤ 145), a famous restaurant set inside a series of
caves high above the gorge. A footpath from the restaurant
leads to another hamlet of cave houses, even more isolated
than the first.

You cannot take a car further than this, but **walkers** can
continue on the road which climbs through almond and

olive groves and forests of Canary pine towards the centre of
the island. This is a magnificent route but it should only be
attempted by experienced walkers with a good map or guide.

TAKING A BREAK

The cave bars at **Cuevas Bermejas** are good for a drink and a
snack, but **Tagoror** (➤ 145) is the best place for lunch.

✚ 184 C5
🚌 11, 21 from Las Palmas, 41, 52 from Maspalomas to Agüimes then take
a taxi

Cave houses
are warm
in winter
and cool in
summer

BARRANCO DE GUAYADEQUE: INSIDE INFO

Top tip Come here on a Sunday, when the restaurant **Tagoror** serves *sancocho*
(Canarian fish stew) and the valley floor fills up with families enjoying a picnic
lunch or an impromptu barbecue in the barranco.

Hidden gem Coming out of the valley, don't miss the opportunity for a stroll
around the old town of **Agüimes** (➤ 138). At the nearby town of Ingenio is the
Museo de Piedra y Artesanía (open Mon–Sat 8–6:30, tel: 928/781-124). Here
you can see the *calados* (open threadwork) and *bondados* (embroidery) for
which this area is famous. It is also possible to buy local handicrafts here.

In more depth If you want to find out more about the Barranco de
Guayadeque, visit the **information centre** on the road to Agüimes (open Tue–Sat
9–5, Sun 10–6).

2 Playa del Inglés

The dusty tomato fields of Playa del Inglés have been transformed into the setting for the richest cash crop Gran Canaria has ever known – tourism. Even if you are not staying here, it is essential to visit to see what tourism has done for Gran Canaria. The once barren clifftops are now a non-stop holiday playground, as big and brash as anything you will find on Tenerife, Mallorca or the Spanish costas. The "English beach" has become an international party circuit of Scandinavian restaurants and German bars, with hotels, apartment blocks, bungalows, shopping centres, playgrounds, minigolf-courses and nightclubs catering for the whims of a year-round stream of visitors.

Beach life

The Paseo Costa Canaria looks out over the real glory of Playa del Inglés. The **beach** of fine golden sand stretches for more than 5km (3 miles), bordering the Dunas de Maspalomas (➤ 130) for much of the way. Watersports, pedal-boats, parasols and sunbeds are all available and there are restaurants and bars.

Tourists stroll along the beach at Playa del Inglés

The central part of the beach is always crowded, but it is usually possible to find a quieter spot, particularly if you head for the long stretch of nudist beach between Maspalomas and Playa del Inglés. The Paseo (promenade) itself makes for an

The South

enjoyable stroll, especially at sunset, and forms the central
section of a longer walk along the south coast (➤ 158).
You can walk directly onto the dunes from the beaches at
Maspalomas and Playa del Inglés, or from the mirador behind
the Riu Palace Maspalomas Hotel (➤ 144).

The night-time lights of Playa del Inglés

The Town

Most people who stay here find that Playa del Inglés provides
everything they want from their holiday, although some may
consider it a rather artificial place, without the historic old
quarter or central square that acts as a focus for most Spanish
towns. The **plazas**, where people meet, are inside the *centros
comerciales* (shopping centres), the best known of which is the
Yumbo (where the tourist office is situated). Others are the
Cita and the Kasbah, which is the focus of young nightlife.

Close to the Kasbah, an attempt has been made to create
a heart for the resort with the opening of the ecumenical
church of San Salvador in 1971. The church is built in
the shape of a ship, with a twisted wrought-iron façade
symbolising a divided Christian church, and an altar hewn
out of red volcanic rock.
Services are held in English,
German and Spanish.

Playa del Inglés is
the biggest resort in
a conurbation which
stretches from San Agustín
to Maspalomas and
beyond. This area has been
successfully rebranded as the
Costa Canaria, in an effort
to dispel some of the negative
connotations of the "English
beach". In fact each resort has
its own particular flavour. San
Agustín is old-fashioned and
upmarket, Playa del Inglés
is young and upfront, while
Las Meloneras, beyond the
lighthouse at Maspalomas, is
a luxury holiday village with

CONDE DE LA VEGA GRANDE
Much of the development of this area is due to
the vision of one man, Alejandro del Castillo,
Conde de la Vega Grande, who turned his
estates into the first tourist developments
along the south coast. Depending on your
point of view, the count is either the hero or
the villain of tourism in Gran Canaria. His
efforts unleashed a building boom which
lasted through the 1960s and 1970s, the
results of which can be seen around Playa del
Inglés. This is a place of high-rise buildings
and wide boulevards, whose names (Inglaterra,
Alemania, Francia, Italia, Finlandia, Estados
Unidos) pay tribute to the resort's international
clientele. Unfortunately the only pleasant place
for walking is along the seafront promenade.

chic hotels, an 18-hole golf course, a conference centre and shopping mall. San Fernando, inland from Playa del Inglés, is where the people who work in the industry live. This is the place for a slice of authentic Spanish life, with neighbourhood shops and tapas bars frequented by locals.

TAKING A BREAK

There are restaurants and bars all over the resort, particularly in the shopping centres, behind the beach and along Avenida de Tirajana. For something authentically Spanish try **Las Cumbres** (➤ 145).

✚ 184 B1 🚍 30 from Las Palmas; numerous buses from all local areas

Tourist information office
✉ Avenida España, Yumbo Centre ☎ 928/771-550 🕐 Jul–Sep Mon–Fri 9–2, 3–8, Sat 9–1; Oct–Jun Mon–Fri 9–9, Sat 9–1

The church of San Salvador has services in three different languages

Templo Ecuménico de San Salvador
✉ Avenida de Italia ☎ 928/770-496 🕐 Daily; check the board outside for service times 💰 Free

---

PLAYA DEL INGLÉS: INSIDE INFO

Top tip Pick up a **local bus map** from the tourist office at the Yumbo centre.
■ Walking around the resort can be quite tiring and **buses** make an economical and energy-conserving alternative.

❸ Dunas de Maspalomas

Eerie, surreal, almost lunar in their simplicity, these Sahara-like sand dunes at the southernmost tip of the island are one of the scenic highlights of Gran Canaria.

These undulating hills and valleys cover an area of 4sq km (1.5 sq miles) between Maspalomas and Playa del Inglés. The sand is composed of finely ground shells, left behind when the sea retreated at the end of the Ice Age. There are few more memorable experiences than walking barefoot across the hot sand and watching the dunes change shape as each new gust of wind creates intricate patterns in the sandscape.

Although access to the dunes is unrestricted, they form part of a protected **nature reserve** and it is essential not to pick plants, disturb wildlife or move stones. Sunbathing is permitted and you will notice that the area is popular with naturists and gay men. Camel rides (➤ 149) are available, starting from the western edge of the dunes, though environmentalists disapprove, claiming that they have an adverse impact on the fragile ecosystem.

Resort Beach

Maspalomas beach is a popular spot. The landmark here is the lighthouse, **Faro de Maspalomas**, which at 56m (184 feet) is the tallest in the Canaries. A promenade lined with shops, restaurants, cafés and luxury hotels leads to **Las Meloneras**, a sheltered bay once frequented by locals but now the site of a luxury hotel built in a traditional Canarian village style.

Follow the footprints across the shifting sands

The neighbouring resort of Maspalomas is mostly low-rise and chic, with bungalows and villas set around gardens. Much of the accommodation is behind the golf course in the district of Campo Internacional. The **Faro 2** shopping centre, the heart of the resort, is also here.

Ecological Concerns

Maspalomas beach has undergone many changes in recent years. When the lighthouse was built in 1886, Maspalomas could only be reached by a dirt track and most of the supplies had to be brought in by boat.

The first plans for tourist development came in the 1950s, with proposals for a *parador* (state-run hotel), zoo and racetrack on what was described as an "isolated beach". The landowner, Conde de la Vega Grande (➤ 128), rejected the plans in favour of large-scale construction, and the battle for the dunes began.

A golf-course, opened in 1968, encroached onto the dunes and the notorious Hotel Dunas was built on the sand before being demolished in 1989.

Ecologists are continuing to campaign against beach bars and camel shelters, but the Dunas de Maspalomas are better protected now than they have ever been since tourism began and a balance

LA CHARCA

At the west end of the dunes, La Charca is a sea-water and freshwater lagoon with reed beds and marshes which hosts a wide variety of nesting and migratory birds. Kestrel, grey heron, seagulls and Kentish plover are all regularly seen here, and the Sardinian warbler nests in the tamarisk groves between February and June. Mullet are found in La Charca at high tide, lizards scramble about the banks and osprey are occasionally spotted searching for fish at dusk. At the mouth of the lagoon, a grove of Canary palm trees extends westward into the area known as El Oasis, home to some of the island's top hotels.

has finally been struck between the conflicting interests of profit and preservation.

Further inland, **Sonnenland** is a new tourist area with views over the dunes, while **El Tablero** is the Canarian quarter of Maspalomas, a village-like suburb on the far side of the motorway with a distinctly Spanish atmosphere.

TAKING A BREAK

The nearest restaurants to the dunes are in the **Oasis shopping centre** in the lanes behind Maspalomas beach. The lunch-time buffet at **La Foresta** (➤ 146) at the Riu Grand Palace (Maspalomas Oasis) hotel is a good deal.

Faro de Maspalomas seen across the sands

🚹 184 A1 🚌 30 from Las Palmas; numerous buses from all local areas

Tourist information office
✉ Avenida Turoperador Tui (Campo Internacional) ☎ 928/769-585
🕐 Mon–Fri 9–2

DUNAS DE MASPALOMAS: INSIDE INFO

Top tips Take plenty of **water** if you plan to walk across the dunes as the combination of sun and sand can be very dehydrating. It is generally easier to walk barefoot. For more advice on walking across the dunes, see the Costa Canaria walk (➤ 158).

- Beyond the Faro de Maspalomas (lighthouse), **Playa de las Mujeres** is a rocky beach with good conditions for surfing and windsurfing.
- One of the best **views** of the dunes is at sunset from the terrace of the Rui Palace Maspalomas hotel in Playa del Inglés (➤ 144).

In more depth The **information centre** for the Dunas de Maspalomas nature reserve has an intersting permanent exhibition on the history and ecology of the dunes. It is situated in Playa del Inglés, behind the Riu Palace Maspalomas hotel by the mirador overlooking the dunes. The centre is open Monday–Saturday but hours are erratic.

You can use the lighthouse to guide your way as you walk across the dunes

④ Palmitos Parque

The squawking of parrots in a verdant valley of palm trees forms the scenic backdrop to Gran Canaria's most popular family attraction. This subtropical park inside the Barranco de Chamoriscán has more than 200 species of birds, including macaws, toucans, hornbills, flamingoes, cockatiels, peacocks and cranes. Among the other attractions are cactus gardens, an orchid house, a butterfly house, reptiles and an aquarium.

Education and Conservation

The park manages to strike a balance between education, conservation and entertainment. Most visitors head straight for the **parrot shows**, which take place 10:30, 11:30, 2:30, 3:30 and 4:30 on a café terrace near the entrance. The parrots have been trained to perform an amazing variety of tricks, from riding bicycles to doing jigsaws, painting pictures and counting to ten. They have even learned how to imitate foreign visitors, lying back on a parrot-size deckchair reading a newspaper. Children love it, most adults may feel slightly uncomfortable, yet the fact is that such popular displays help to fund serious conservation programmes among the many endangered species which exist in the park.

It is best to follow the signs around the park to see everything in the suggested order. The complete circuit takes about an hour of leisurely walking, but you should allow half a day. Don't miss the excellent **birds of prey show** which takes place twice daily (12 and 2) in an amphitheatre on a hilltop overlooking the park, where eagles, owls and peregrine falcons swoop down over the audience in free flight. Other

A collection of *Echinocacus grusonii* among other cacti in the park

It's not just for parrots – the park also features butterflies and plants

highlights are the **cactus garden** with its numerous cactus and aloe plants, among them *silla de la suegra* or "mother-in-law's chair"; the aquarium with sea-water and freshwater tanks of tropical fish; and **gibbon island**, home to a pair of gibbons.

A shop at the exit sells colourful souvenirs such as T-shirts and stuffed toy parrots, and there is also the opportunity to have your photo taken with a pair of screeching macaws.

TAKING A BREAK

There are **cafés** and **ice-cream kiosks** throughout the park, and a **self-service terrace** near the exit which serves soup, salads and hot meals. Alternatively, take a **picnic**.

➕ 183 E3 ✉ Barranco de los Palmitos, 15km (9 miles) northwest of Playa del Inglés ☎ 928/140-276; www.palmitospark.es 🕐 Daily 10–6 🚌 45 from Playa del Inglés, 70 from Puerto Rico 💵 Expensive

---

PALMITOS PARQUE: INSIDE INFO

Top tips There are regular **buses** to Palmitos Parque from Playa del Inglés, departing every 20 minutes during the morning and every 30 minutes during the afternoon. There are also four buses each morning from Puerto Rico and Maspalomas, returning in the afternoon.

■ **Children** love Palmitos Parque, but there is a fair amount of walking involved, so it is best to take a pushchair for younger children.

■ Pick up a **plant guide** at the entrance to help you to identify the various plants on display.

Hidden gem Don't miss the **hummingbirds** as you leave the park. These tiny birds with their bright plumage and unbelievably fast wing movements live in a series of small cages near the exit.

In more depth After devastating fires swept through the centre of Gran Canaria in 2007, the park was closed in need of major renovations, but in August 2008 it reopened once again restored to its former glory.

5 Puerto de Mogán

An enticing blend of fishing village, marina and chic holiday resort, Puerto de Mogán is often held up as a model of sympathetic tourist development in Gran Canaria. Low-rise villas with hand-painted borders and gardens of hibiscus and bougainvillea form a gentle backdrop to the harbour, where Venetian-style bridges arch over sea-water canals. New development is gradually emerging back behind the waterfront, but it is less intrusive than in other resorts, and the low-rise apartments, a luxury hotel and a scattering of shops blend perfectly into the mountain landscape.

Chic Resort

This is the farthest place on the island from Las Palmas and it marks the western limit of tourism. Puerto de Mogán was not developed for tourism until the 1980s, and so it was able to avoid some of the excesses of its neighbours along the coast. Right from the start, this was a small-scale, exclusive resort, designed for the sort of people who could afford a berth in the harbour. Others have had to make do with seeing Puerto de Mogán on a day trip by boat from Puerto Rico (► 141).

Most people come here to wander around the waterside, admiring the yachts and the fishing vessels and enjoying the view from waterfront cafés. If you stroll to the end of the harbour, to the El Faro bar/restaurant, there is a good view out to sea. Whales and dolphins are a common sight, but the best way to spot them is to take a boat trip from the waterfront.

For something more active, diving, sailing and fishing trips are all on offer, and an added attraction is a journey on a yellow submarine (tel: 928/565-108) a 45-minute voyage to

PUERTO DE MOGÁN: INSIDE INFO

Top tips The **Friday morning market** is a good place to find lace tablecloths, leather sandals and Senegalese drums.

■ Puerto de Mogán is a very different place at **night**, when the day visitors have gone home and the locals promenade around the harbour and play dominoes in the Plaza del Sol. From the cliffs at the western end of the port there is a fine **view** of the sun setting over Tenerife.

Hidden gem Climb up above the port to the small **traditional village** of whitewashed houses on a slope where the fishermen live. The authenticity of this village contrasts sharply with the glitziness of the port.

the bottom of the ocean to observe marine life and the wreck of a freighter lying 20m (65 feet) below the surface (for bookings, tel: 928/565-108). Come evening, when the crowds have gone, only the breeze stirring the rigging of the boats in the harbour disturbs the quiet and peaceful air of the town. The mountains form the perfect backdrop.

High-Rise Hotels

From the small sandy beach you can see **Playa de Taurito**, a sharp contrast to Puerto de Mogán. Here, big hotels have grown up around landscaped gardens and a sea-water lake in a ravine between the cliffs. If you prefer a more isolated beach and are prepared for a long but pleasant walk, a dirt track westwards from the village leads to the next beach at Veneguera (➤ 141).

Flower-decked houses in Puerto de Mogán's streets

Inland

A road leads inland along the floor of the **Barranco de Mogán**, a valley where mangoes, avocados and papaya are grown. Outsize coffee pots, stools and household utensils line the road, kept here throughout the year and transported on carriages in a ritual procession during the feast of San Antonio de Padua each June (➤ 149). After 12km (7 miles) the road reaches **Mogán**, a county town in the shadow of the Guirre mountain. The main sight here is the church of San Antonio, containing a fine hand-carved wooden coffered ceiling.

TAKING A BREAK

Left: The fishing fleet in the harbour at Puerto de Mogán

Keep walking around the marina until you come to the fishing harbour, where **Restaurante Cofradía** (➤ 146) serves fresh local fish. The nearby **El Faro** is a popular spot (for its views more than its food) in a lighthouse at the end of the waterside.

➕ 182 B3 🚌 1 from Las Palmas, 32 from Playa del Inglés, 84 from Puerto de Mogán to Mogán

At Your Leisure

6 Agüimes

The historic centre of this town, once the seat of the bishops of Gran Canaria, has been sympathetically restored as a model of the new, inland tourism which the island is trying so hard to promote. The narrow streets around the main square, **Plaza del Rosario**, are full of old-style, whitewashed houses, several of them converted into holiday homes. The plaza is dominated by the neo-classical church of San Sebastián, a former cathedral with sculptures by Canarian artist, Luján Pérez. Agüimes is a thriving town with a strong Canarian identity, and a commitment to the arts which embraces festivals of drama, storytelling and music (➤ 149).

The nearby sand and pebble beach at **Arinaga** is good for windsurfing and dinghy sailing, and the Bahia de Formas attracts migrating birds.

✚ 185 D4 🚍 11, 21 from Las Palmas, 41 from Maspalomas

7 Barranco de Fataga

The biggest gorge on Gran Canaria is also one of the most dramatic, with palm-filled oases, walls of honey-coloured rock, and canyon-like scenery that conjures up images of Wild West films.

The road into the gorge begins in Playa del Inglés and for visitors staying on the south coast the drive up to Fataga is the easiest way to get a brief taste of Gran Canaria's mountain scenery. The first stop is **Mundo Aborigen**, an open-air theme park devoted to the Guanche way of life. Although it lacks the scholarship of the Museo Canario (➤ 52), the park gives genuine insight into the pre-Hispanic culture of Gran Canaria, brought to life through a series of tableaux and the chronicles of the early Spanish conquistadors. There are reproductions of stone houses, burial caves, a convent and a meeting place, and vivid descriptions of everything from surgery to execution.

Just north of here, a bend in the road is the setting for a magnificent *mirador*, with views over the canyon and back towards the coast. There is a bar and a small car park where you can get out and stretch your legs while taking in the views.

The road continues to **Arteara**, where camel rides are offered in the oasis. At the end of the Fataga valley, a short climb up a

A walk around the old quarter of Agüimes offers a chance to explore a different side of Gran Canaria

Whitewashed houses in Fataga sit among palm trees and prickly pears and in the background are the mountains of Pico de las Neives

cactus-covered hillside leads to a Guanche necropolis, where many of the tombs are still intact.

After more twists and turns you arrive in **Fataga**, extensively restored as a showpiece village of traditional Canarian houses surrounded by orchards and palm trees. There are several bars and cafés. The German artist Friedhelm Berghorn has a studio at the top of the village and there are craft and souvenir shops on the main road. The shady square in front of the church makes a good place to relax and prepare yourself for the hair-raising drive back down the gorge.

➕ 184 A2

Mundo Aborigen
✉ Carretera de Fataga, km6 ☎ 928/172-295
🕐 Daily 9–6 🚌 18 from Playa del Inglés/Maspalomas 💷 Expensive

🔟 Arguineguín
Until recently this small town was little more than a fishing village. It is still a working fishing port, with smacks tied up in the harbour, a shrine to the Virgin of Fishermen,

BOAT TRIPS
Puerto Rico (▶ 141) is the starting point for a number of boat trips. They can all be booked through tour operators or at the desks in the harbour. The cheapest are the Lineas Salmón (www.lineasalmon.com) ferry services, which depart every hour for Puerto de Mogán and for Arguineguín.

Several companies offer dolphin-watching cruises from Puerto Rico, including *Spirit of the Sea* (tel: 928/150-010; www.dolphin-whale. com), whose two-hour trip, three times daily, on a glass-bottomed catamaran uses sophisticated searching equipment, though sightings are not guaranteed. A percentage of the revenue from ticket sales contributes to research into dolphins and whales, carried out by the marine scientists on board.

Daytime and sunset cruises, with food, drink, entertainment and swimming included, are available on the schooner *Timanfaya* (tel: 928/268-280; www.velerotimanfayo. com). For a more laid-back cruise, the 30m (100-foot) *Super Cat* (tel: 928/735-656) catamaran sails daily up the west coast to Güigüi

Yachts and motor boats moored in the marina built into a protected bay in the resort of Puerto Rico

OFF THE BEATEN TRACK

The road into the Barranco de Arguineguín begins opposite a banana plantation where the coast road divides from the motorway. North on the GC505 to the village of Cerado Espino, it climbs into a fertile valley of tropical fruits around the hamlet of Barranquillo de San Andrés. A right fork leads to Soria, where the restaurant Casa Fernando serves hearty Canarian food at good prices.

From here you can walk down to the dam overlooking the Soria reservoir, built in 1971 to provide water for the south coast resorts. The road through Soria quickly deteriorates into a dusty track; if you have an off-road vehicle, you can continue for 8km (5 miles) to Cruce de la Data, returning through Ayacata and the Barranco de Fataga.

several good seafood restaurants and some lively fishermen's bars, but it has gradually expanded to become a mass-market resort popular with Germans and Scandinavians. A coastal promenade connects Arguineguín to Patalavaca, where luxury hotels and apartments are springing up around the beaches and coves and **Anfi del Mar**, an up-market timeshare resort with a beach of imported Caribbean sand. The walk takes around an hour.

Arguineguín is busy every Tuesday and Thursday as it hosts one of the region's biggest **markets**. You can take one of the regular boat services from Puerto Rico or Puerto de Mogán for a stroll around the harbour and lunch by the water.

🕂 183 D1 🚌 1, 91 from Las Palmas; 32 from Playa del Inglés and Puerto de Mogán

9 Puerto Rico

The first sight of Puerto Rico takes your breath away. Rows of white apartment blocks climb up the steep hillsides, so high that you need a taxi to get to the top and there is even talk of putting in a cable car.

The resort is especially popular with British families. As it was built in the 1970s, there is no historic centre, but its heart is the large park inside the *barranco* (gorge), planted with palm and ficus trees and featuring mini-golf courses, tennis courts, a playground and a waterpark. The main shopping centre is just behind the park, and there is another at the top of the hill.

The beach is a crescent of golden sand imported from the Sahara. The sand shelves gently into the sea, making it perfect for young children. From the harbours to either side of

the beach, boards advertise fishing trips, watersports, cruises and ferries to Puerto de Mogán (➤ 136). A clifftop path leads in around 20 minutes to **Playa de los Amadores**, where there is another glorious artificial beach. From the path there are good sunset views over Tenerife. (Tourist information ➤ 37.)

🟥 182 C2 🚌 1, 91 from Las Palmas; 32 from Playa del Inglés and Puerto de Mogán

10 West Coast Beaches

The remote beaches of the southwest coast are largely untouched by tourism, though after a long legal and political battle **Playa de Veneguera** (🟥 182 B3) has been sold to developers and may be transformed into a mega-resort by 2010. At the moment it can only be reached by a 10km (6-mile) dirt track through orchards and banana plantations, and

---

FOR KIDS

Although the children may be happy just playing on the beach, there are lots of other attractions to keep them entertained. The top draw for families is **Palmitos Parque** (➤ 134), though **Cocodrilo Park** near Agüimes (tel: 928/784-725, open Mon–Fri and Sun 10–5) features crocodile and parrot shows and also has tigers, monkeys and deer. Or try the **Mundo Aborigen** (➤ 138) and **Sioux City** (near San Agustín, tel: 928/762-573; www.siouxcity-grancanaria.com) theme parks, and the ride on the *Yellow Submarine* at Puerto de Mogán (➤ 136). **Aqualand** (tel: 928/140-525; www.aqualand.es, open daily 10–5/6), on the road to Palmitos Parque and Atlantico (tel: 902/452-525, open daily 10–6) in Puerto Rico, offer slides, rides and thrills. **Holiday World**, in the Campo Internacional area of Maspalomas (tel: 928/154-777; www.holidayworld-maspalomas.com, open daily 6–midnight), is an old-fashioned funfair and amusement park.

is inaccessible without an off-road vehicle. Seek out this lonely beach of black sand before it is too late.

Playa de Tasarte (✚ 182 B3) is situated at the mouth of a *barranco* (gorge) and has the advantage that it can be reached by a tarmac road. A simple fish restaurant on the seafront is popular with locals at weekends.

The best of all the remote beaches is **Güigüi** (pronounced *wee-wee*; (✚ 182 A5), which can only be reached by a 3-hour hike over the mountains from Tasártico or by boat from Puerto Rico. It is a protected nature reserve and perhaps the most idyllic spot in Gran Canaria.

⑪ Puerto de la Aldea

This small fishing village is also the port for the tomato town of **San Nicolás de Tolentino**, 5km (3 miles) inland. There is a long pebble beach with good surf at its southern end, and a small sheltered beach of dark sand beneath overhanging rocks by the harbour. There are a couple of good fish restaurants at the end of the promenade.

Puerto de la Aldea is Gran Canaria's westernmost point and it can feel quite wild in winter when the wind gets up. The lagoon at the southern end of the beach is the setting for one of Gran Canaria's oldest festivals, **Fiesta del Charco** (➤ 149).

✚ 178 A2 🚌 38 from Puerto de Mogán to San Nicolás

CACTUALDEA CACTUS PARK
This unusual park near Tocodomán, San Nicolas de Torentino (tel: 928/789-057, open daily 10–6, moderate) combines an impressive cactus garden with tourist attractions including a model Guanche cave and a carillon. There is an amphitheatre with displays of pole-vaulting and Canarian wrestling. The restaurant serves typical Canarian cuisine. As well as cacti, the gardens have palm and dragon trees and are worth a visit if you don't have time to visit the Jardín Canario (➤ 81).

The pebble beach at Puerto de la Aldea is an excellent place to enjoy a lunch of freshly caught fish

Where to...
Stay

Prices

The symbols refer to the average cost of a double room in high season, generally November to April. All prices exclude 4.5 per cent sales tax (IGIC).

€ under €70   **€€** €70–€130   **€€€** over €130

AGÜIMES

Casa de los Camellos €€

A 300-year-old stone barn in the town centre has become a hotel, whose 12 rooms with traditional wooden balconies are set around interior courtyards and gardens. Agüimes has become something of a centre for rural tourism in Gran Canaria, and several houses have been converted into *casas rurales* (▶ 40). Award-winning restaurant.
🚹 185 D4 🖂 Calle El Progreso 12
☎ 928/785-003

peacocks and hens. The restaurant serves Canarian mountain cuisine on a poolside terrace.
🚹 184 B4 🖂 Carretera de Fataga a San Bartolomé, km1 ☎ 928/172-089;
www.molinodeagua.es

MASPALOMAS

Grand Hotel Residencia €€€

This small designer hotel has quickly become established as one of the most exclusive addresses on the island. Rooms are set around the pool inside Spanish-Moorish villas with wooden balconies and colonial-style furnishings. Breakfast is served buffet-style and the dinner menu features Canarian specialities and international cuisine. Added touches include internet access and CD players in the rooms, and copies of artist Joan Miró's works on the walls.
🚹 183 F1 🖂 Avenida del Oasis 32
☎ 928/723-100; www.grand-hotel-residencia.com

BARRANCO DE FATAGA

Molino del Agua de Fataga €€

This rural hotel is situated in a magnificent palm grove, in a group of converted farm buildings overlooking the restored *gofio* mill from which it takes its name. The rooms are decorated in traditional style, with iron furniture made by a blacksmith who works on the premises. Rooms are small, simple and pretty, with a wooden balcony or terrace. Camel rides are available, and a playground has goats,

H10 Playa Meloneras Palace €€€

In a quiet, elevated spot overlooking the sea next to the Meloneras golf course, the hotel is an unusual design, built in typical Canarian stone and set in attractive gardens. A stunning high-arched ceiling dominates the spacious reception. The restaurant offers a variety of delicacies in a cosy environment and the hotel also has a cocktail bar for relaxing after a long day sightseeing, walking or simply relaxing on the beach.

The 350 air-conditioned bedrooms and 23 suites are well furnished and equipped with all the amenities you would expect in a luxury hotel. Take a dip in one of the hotel's two swimming pools, relax in the Jacuzzi or be pampered and beautified at the Wellness health and beauty centre.
🚹 183 E1 🖂 C/ Mar Caspio 5, Urbanización Las Meloneras ☎ 928/128-282;
www.h10hotels.com

€€ €70–€130

Riu Grand Palace (Maspalomas Oasis) €€€

Considered the top hotel on the south coast, the Maspalomas Oasis has 65,000sq m (16 acres) of gardens in the heart of the Oasis palm grove. Sunloungers are scattered throughout the grounds, where peacocks strut and guests practise their ping-pong and putting. This has all the facilities you would expect of a five-star hotel, including 24-hour room service, evening entertainment and satellite TV, as well as a billiards room, children's club and special touches, such as occasional summer barbecues by the lake.
+ 183 F1 ⊠ Playa de Maspalomas ☎ 928/141-448; www.riu.com

Riu Palace Meloneras €€€

This huge complex of 305 hotel rooms and 144 villas was the first to open in the new resort of Las Meloneras. The tone is set by the extravagant lobby, all cut-glass chandeliers and polished stone.

The extensive gardens feature two swimming pools and a children's pool, a play area and access to the seafront promenade. The beach at Maspalomas is a short walk away. Hotel facilities include a health and beauty centre, tennis, table tennis and a gym.
+ 183 E1 ⊠ Urbanización Las Meloneras ☎ 928/143-182; www.riu.com

PLAYA DEL INGLÉS

Riu Palace Maspalomas €€€

On the edge of the Maspalomas sand dunes, this imposing hotel has all the appearance of a Moorish palace. It has 368 rooms and facilities include three pools, a whirlpool, beauty salon and an elegant shopping arcade. A short walk over the dunes leads to the beach, a longer trek to the lighthouse at Maspalomas. Many of the rooms offer great sunset vistas of the dunes.
+ 184 B1 ⊠ Avenida de Tirajana ☎ 928/769-500; www.riu.com

PUERTO DE MOGÁN

Hotel Cordial Mogán Playa €€€

A stunning hotel in one of the better Gran Canaria resorts. Its exterior is in traditional colonial style, with a dramatic mountain backdrop and lush tropical gardens. The reception area is striking, with a huge stained-glass dome in the centre and a little bridge over a pool, complete with cascading waterfall. The facilities are first rate and include the Los Guayres à la carte restaurant, a wellness centre and pools with an artificial beach. Keep an eye on bargains via the internet to experience luxury at a reasonable price.
+ 182 B3 ⊠ Avenida de los Marrero, Playa de Mogán ☎ 928/724-100; www.cordialcanarias.com

Hotel Puerto de Mogan €€

Formerly the Club de Mar, this small hotel on the waterside has 56 double rooms as well as 90 apartments in the villas behind

the port. All the apartments have a roof-top sun terrace and access to hotel facilities including the pool. From the pool area you can dive straight into the sea off the small beach. If the hotel is full, several waterfront bars and cafés have villas and apartments for rent.
+ 182 B3 ⊠ Playa de Mogán ☎ 928/565-066; www.hotelpuertodemogan.com

SAN AGUSTÍN

Gloria Palace €€

This hotel has the largest thalassotherapy centre in Europe, with five sea-water pools and treatments ranging from seaweed therapy to Chinese acupuncture and ultrasonic marine baths.
There is a 15-minute walk to the beach, across a main road, though there is a courtesy bus available. A panoramic restaurant specialises in Basque and French cuisine.
+ 184 B2 ⊠ Las Margaritas ☎ 928/268-603 or 128-505; www.hotelgloriapalace.com

Where to...
Eat and Drink

Prices
Expect to pay per person for a meal, excluding drinks and service
€ under €15   €€ €15–€30   €€€ over €30

Most restaurants on Gran Canaria are open throughout the year, though they may close for an annual holiday, at some time during the year.

BARRANCO DE GUAYADEQUE

Tagoror €€
The most memorable feature of this restaurant is its setting in cool caves high above the *barranco*. Eat outside on a vine-covered terrace. The food is typically Canarian – grilled meats, spicy potatoes, *morcilla* sausage and local *quesos* (cheeses).

Desserts include fried bananas with *bienmesabe* (almond syrup). It gets busy at weekends, especially on Sunday when locals gather to eat *sancocho* (fish stew).
🕂 174 C5 ⬚ Montaña de las Tierras ☎ 928/172-013; www.restaurante-tagoror.com 🕘 Daily 10am–midnight

SAN AGUSTÍN

Gorbea €€€
Take the lift from the hotel lobby to the ninth floor for excellent Basque-French cuisine and panoramic views of San Agustin beach and the

Dunes of Maspalomas. Specialities on the menu include asparagus wrapped in salmon and filled with seafood, peppered turbot *a la salsa rosa* and lamb cutlets a la Segoviana.
🕂 184 B2 ⬚ Hotel Gloria Palace, Calle Las Margaritas ☎ 928/128-500; www.hotelgloriapalace.com 🕘 Mon–Sat 7–midnight

PLAYA DEL INGLÉS

La Casa Vieja €€–€€€
Those who enjoy chargrilled meat and traditional Canarian food should try this rustic Canarian house. The *parillada* of assorted meats is flame-cooked on an open grill and the bread is really tasty served with *alioli* (garlic mayonnaise). La Casa Vieja is located a little way out on the road to Fataga, on the left as you come up the hill. A Canarian band often entertain with traditional music.
🕂 184 B1 ⬚ El Lomo 139, Carretera a Fataga ☎ 928/762-736 🕘 Daily 1pm–midnight

Las Cumbres Canarias €€
With so much bland international cuisine on offer, this distinctively Spanish cellar restaurant in the heart of town is a surprise. Shepherds' crooks and sheeps' bells give a clue to the speciality – roast lamb. The main influence comes from La Rioja, in dishes like roast peppers and salt cod, but other Spanish regions are represented.
🕂 184 B1 ⬚ Edificio Taida, Avenida de Tirajana 9 ☎ 928/760-941 🕘 Daily 1–4, 7–midnight. Closed Apr–end Jun

Rias Bajas €€€
For something a little more upmarket, seek out this pristine basement restaurant, decorated in cool blue tones. It's all about fish and seafood, and the dishes are influenced by the Galician region; the *zarzuela* fish and seafood casserole is a popular option.
🕂 184 B1 ⬚ Edificio Playa del Sol, Avenida de Tirajana ☎ 928/764-033; www.riasbajas-playadelingles.com 🕘 Daily 1–4, 7–midnight

MASPALOMAS

Ciao–Ciao €€–€€€

One of the most popular beach-side restaurants in Meloneras is Italian owned and run. Opt to eat outside or in the plush dining room with high-backed wicker chairs and exotic floral decorations on the tables. The waiters are happy to help you choose from the interesting pasta dishes on the menu, and there is a selection of meat and fish dishes.

+ 183 F1 **CC Meloneras, local 128–129** **928/146-969** **Daily 9am–midnight**

La Foresta €€–€€€

Non-residents are welcome at the poolside restaurant of the Riu Grand Palace (Maspalomas Oasis) hotel, and the lunchtime buffet is good value. The full menu will leave quite a hole in your wallet, but you can skip the main course and opt for the salad and dessert buffet. After lunch, stroll around the gardens or sit beneath the palm trees.

+ 183 F1 **Hotel Riu Grand Palace, Playa de Maspalomas** **928/141-448** **Daily 1–3pm**

Grill Faro €€–€€€

On the seafront promenade protected from the sea breeze by glass screens, Grill Faro offers attractively presented Canarian cuisine, plus pizza and pasta choices, served with a friendly banter. You can watch the chef at work in an open kitchen.

+ 183 F1 **CC Boulevard Faro** **928/145-379; www.restaurantgrillfaro.com** **Daily 9am–midnight**

PUERTO DE MOGÁN

La Bodeguilla Juananá €€€

This chic little tavern on the harbourside square offers new Canarian cuisine. They do everything with an artistic flourish, from the carved wooden seats to the big ceramic plates and the enormous handwritten menu boards brought to your table. The speciality is a selection of Canarian cheeses, served plain, steeped in olive oil or cooked in white wine. Other local ingredients turn up in unexpected ways, such as smoked swordfish with avocado followed by *gofio* ice-cream with palm honey for dessert. All of the wines served are produced on the island.

+ 182 B3 **Local 390** **928/565-044** **Daily 7pm–midnight (but can be erratic)**

La Caracola: Seemuschel €€€

German owners Chris and Dieter are passionate about their delightful little fish restaurant overlooking the harbour, and will ensure you have an enjoyable meal. Crisp ice-blue tablecloths lap with sparking cutlery and glass set off against brilliant white walls provide an ideal setting for chef Dieter to perform his magic using only the very best fish. Only room for 14 so reservations are a must.

+ 182 B3 **Local X-12 2, Harbour Puerto Mogán** **928/565-486; www.seemuschel. com** **Mon–Sat 7–11; closed Sep–May**

Restaurante Cofradía €€

The fishermen's cooperative by the harbour has the freshest fish in town. The place where local fishermen gathered during the day is smarter but still has a lively Spanish atmosphere. There are tables are outside on a bamboo-covered terrace with waterside views. Bread is served warm from the oven, with tomatoes, garlic and *alioli* (garlic mayonnaise). Grilled fish comes with a generous helping of vegetables. The more creative dishes are cooked in a new stainless-steel open kitchen.

+ 182 B3 **Dársena Exterior del Puerto** **928/565-321** **Daily 10–10**

ARGUINEGUÍN

Bar Cofradía de Pescadores €€

Tucked away at the end of the harbour, this is a beautifully simple harbourside restaurant. The checked tablecloths, fishing nets and posters of Atlantic fish are a reminder of the days when

Where to...
Shop

Arguineguín was little more than a fishing village. It is run by the fishermen's cooperative and situated at the end of a fish-packing warehouse. Local families come here at weekends and the restaurant has built up a considerable reputation. There's fresh fish straight from the harbour, or paella.

🕈 183 D1 ⌖ Puerto de Arguineguín
☎ 928/150-963 ⏰ Thu–Tue 10am–11pm. Closed Sep

PUERTO RICO

La Cantina €€–€€€

The owner has amassed a huge selection of wines from all over Spain and beyond. This is mostly a place to meet before dinner for a glass of champagne or sherry and a plate of ham, cheese or foie gras, but they also do prime grilled steaks and fondues. Make sure to take a look at the impressive wine cellar.

🕈 182 C2 ⌖ Apartamentos El Greco, Calle Doreste y Molina ☎ 928/560-356 ⏰ Daily 6pm–late

SHOPPING CENTRES

Away from the beach, resort life revolves around the *centros comerciales* – shopping centres by day and entertainment centres at night. These have supermarkets, souvenir shops and news-stands as well as shops selling alcohol, tobacco, perfume, electronics, cameras, watches and leather at duty-free prices. The quality is not always high, but prices are often negotiable and there are genuine bargains to be found.

Playa del Inglés alone has around 13 shopping centres. The Cita has more than 200 shops with an abundance of jewellery, leather, shoes and designer clothes. Other

popular centres include the Yumbo, Kasbah and Metro (▶ 148). Maspalomas has a selection of more sophisticated centres, the largest being Faro 2. Other chic centres are El Faro, Veradero and the most recent, Las Dunas.

ARTS AND CRAFTS

Fedac, inside the tourist information office at Playa del Inglés, is a government-sponsored craft shop selling Canarian handicrafts, such as pottery, lace and musical instruments. Prices are fixed but the quality is guaranteed. Juanana, on the harbourside at Puerto de Mogán, is a quirky bodega (wine shop) and craft shop

where you can buy Canarian wines and cheeses as well as local artwork and ceramics. Also located on the waterfront in Puerto de Mogán, Rincón Canario has a more conventional range of souvenirs.

Inland, there are craft shops in the village of Fataga and also in Ingenio, where the Museo de Piedras y Artesanía Canaria sells local embroidery and other crafts.

MARKETS

The large weekly markets at Arguineguín (Tue and Thu), Puerto de Mogán (Fri) and Playa del Inglés (Mon/Sat) are primarily designed for tourists, with stalls selling leather, lace, inexpensive clothing and shoes, beachwear, beach towels, African carvings and drums at reasonable prices.

Although some of the stalls at these markets are "fixed price", at most stalls the initial asking price is inflated and you are expected to strike a bargain.

Where to...
Be Entertained

MUSIC AND DRAMA

To find out what's on in any particular area, check the listings in the newspapers or ask at the tourist offices in Puerto Rico, Maspalomas or Playa del Inglés.

Concerts are held at the Las Tirajanas Auditorium, which opened in 2000 inside the new convention centre at Las Meloneras.

Look out too for **open-air events**, including an Atlantic music festival on the beach at Playa del Inglés (Jan), a jazz festival in Puerto de Mogán (Mar and Jul) and a song festival at Veneguera (Sep).

Agüimes

Agüimes is the venue for the **Encuentro Tres Continentes** (Three Continents Festival), which brings together theatre groups from Europe, Africa and America for a feast of drama and street theatre each September.

The same town also hosts an annual festival of Spanish and Latin American storytellers in January.

NIGHTLIFE

For many, the nightlife of the south coast resorts is one of the reasons for a holiday in Gran Canaria.

Maspalomas

For those who just want to chill out for a while before hitting the resort's serious clubs, **Club Costa Gabana**, on the seafront promenade at Maspalomas, is a relaxing bar with a chic orange and black interior. A glass-fronted terrace with heaters allows you to enjoy a cocktail overloooking the sea while you listen to live music.

Playa del Inglés

Most of the action takes place in the big shopping centres of Playa del Inglés, especially the area around the **Kasbah** and **Yumbo** centres. The bars start to fill up early in the evening, reaching a peak around midnight, when most people move on to the all-night discos and clubs. Hotspots to watch out for are Chinawhite and Chic/Cream (both in the Kasbah).

The **Cita** centre is another popular area, with large numbers of German bars and drag shows in the central plaza.

Gay Nightlife

The focus of gay nightlife in Gran Canaria is the **Yumbo** centre in Playa del Inglés, which features more than 50 gay bars, clubs and saunas. During the day this is a family-oriented shopping centre, with street musicians and portrait

IN-HOUSE ENTERTAINMENT

- Much of the entertainment in the south of the island takes place in tourist hotels, with discos, karaoke nights, flamenco shows and children's activities.
- Tour operators also lay on a wide range of daytime and evening entertainments, from camel safaris to more relaxed champagne cruises and cabaret shows to Wild West nights.
- There is very little that is authentically Spanish or Canarian about any of these, but if you don't mind letting your hair down with your fellow tourists, they can be good fun and children are usually well catered for.
- Food and drink is often included in the price and audience participation is encouraged.

painters doing brisk business, but after about 10pm the gay character of the Yumbo starts to assert itself.

Casino

At the casino inside the **Meliá Tamarindos Hotel** in San Agustín men are expected to wear a jacket and tie, and a passport is also required.

The casino is open daily 9pm to 4am (8–4 in winter). A number of tour operators arrange evening excursions to the casino, including a dinner show and cabaret.

FESTIVALS

Día de los Reyes (5 Jan): the eve of Epiphany is marked by a street parade in Agüimes, when the Three Wise Men distribute Christmas gifts to the children of the town.

Carnival (Feb): processions, masked dances and extravagant costumes on the streets of Agüimes and Playa del Inglés during the riotous build-up to Lent.

Semana Santa (Mar/Apr): Holy Week procession in historic Agüimes includes sacred icons and religious sculptures.

Día de las Islas Canarias (30 May): Canary Islands' Day is marked by expressions of popular culture, such as wrestling and folk-dancing displays. This is also the feast day of San Fernando, a suburb of Playa del Inglés.

San Antonio de Padua (weekend before 13 Jun): a traditional pilgrimage in Puerto de Mogán in honour of the patron saint, together with a folklore festival and religious processions.

La Virgen del Carmen (16 Jul): processions of fishing boats in Arguineguín, Puerto de Mogán and Puerto de la Aldea in honour of the Virgin Mary, the patron saint of fishermen.

Fiesta del Charco (around 10 Sep): one of the oldest celebrations on Gran Canaria. In the past the inhabitants of San Nicolás de Tolentino (▲ 142) would bathe naked in the charco (lagoon) at Puerto de la Aldea, but when this was banned by the church they took to wading in fully clothed, fishing with their bare hands and splashing each other with water. There is also a **Bajada de la Rama**, similar to that held in Puerto de las Nieves, in which villagers thrash the sea with branches in an effort to bring rain.

Nuestra Señora del Rosario (5 Oct): stick fights, Canarian wrestling, plough-pulling contests, folk dancing, a battle of flowers and the scattering of water and gofio are all elements of this traditional festival in Agüimes (▲ 138).

Navidad (25 Dec): a popular nativity play is staged on Christmas evening at Veneguera.

OUTDOOR ACTIVITIES

Camel Trekking

Camel safaris are available in the Maspalomas sand dunes and the Barranco de Fataga. The main centres are La Baranda in the village of **Fataga** (tel: 928/798-680), Manolo's at **Arteara** (tel: 928/798-686) and Camello Safari Dunas at **Maspalomas** (tel: 928/760-781; www.camellosafaris.com). Some operators offer camel-trekking, usually combined with a meal at a ranch or tea in a Berber-style tent.

Cycling

Touring bikes, mountain bikes, bikes with trailers for children and helmets are all available from **Happy Biking** (Hotel Continental, Avenida de Italia 2, Playa del Inglés, tel: 928/766-832; www.happy-biking.com).

Fishing

The south offers a large choice for sport fishing. **Deep-sea fishing** trips depart from the harbour at Puerto Rico (▲ 141). Most trips leave at around 9am, returning at 3pm, though some operators also offer sunset trips. Advance booking is essential. Freshwater angling is possible in the mountain reservoirs.

Go-karting

The **Gran Karting Club** at San Agustín claims to be the largest in Europe, with separate tracks for adults, teenagers and young children (on the GC500 at Tarajalillo, just outside San Agustín on the road to Las Palmas, tel: 928/157-190; www.grankarting.com, open Oct–Apr daily 10–9; May–Sep 11–10, expensive).

Golf

The oldest established golf-course in the south is at **Maspalomas** (tel: 928/ 762-581; www. maspalomasgolf.net). This 18-hole course on the edge of the dunes offers club rental, driving-range, putting-green and restaurant. A second course opened at **El Salobre** (tel: 928/010-103; www. salobregolfresort.com), off the GC1 motorway near Arguineguín, and another at **Tauro** (tel: 928/128-840; www.anfitauro.es. The newest course is at **Meloneras** (tel: 928/145-309; www.lopeshotels.com).

Horse-riding

Riding lessons and excursions are available at **Happy Horse** on the road to Palmitos Parque (tel: 679/867-057; www.happy-horse.org).

Hipisur in Maspalomas (tel: 928/143-146) offers excursions to the beach or to the mountains. Both excursions are for beginners and experienced riders.

Jeep safaris

Tour operators in resorts offer jeep safaris in the mountains, travelling through the **barrancos** (gorges) in off-road vehicles. You are not usually expected to drive but whether you are a driver or a passenger, you need adequate insurance. If you don't want to hire a car, this is a memorable way to experience some of Gran Canaria's most dramatic scenery. Be prepared to get dusty, dirty and hot.

Book through **Discovery Jeep** Safari (tel: 928/775-188 or 616/070-682, expensive but lunch included).

Tennis and squash

A number of hotels have the luxury of their own tennis courts. There are public tennis and squash courts at the Maspalomas golf course and in the park beside the bus stop at Puerto Rico.

Walking

Guided walks in the mountains are offered by **Free Motion** (tel: 928/777-479; www.free-motion.net), whose offices are inside the Sandy Beach hotel at Playa del Inglés. All tours take all day long, and minibus transfers are included. Take good shoes, water and a picnic. Another company offering guided walks is **Canari Aventura** also in Playa del Inglés (tel: 670/777-343, www. canariaventura.com). Other activities include kayaking, bungee jumping and climbing.

Watersports

Windsurfing, sailing, jet-skiing and diving are available at all of the main resorts.

Experienced **windsurfers** should head for Pozo Izquierdo on the southeast coast or Playa del Águila at San Agustín, where the family of former world champion Björn Dunkerbeck runs a windsurfing school (tel: 928/ 762-978).

Scuba diving courses can be booked with **Davy Jones Diving** at Playa de Arinaga (tel: 699/721-584), Aquanauts at Puerto Rico (tel: 928/560-655; ww.aquanauts-divecentre.com) and Top Diving at Puerto Rico (www.topdiving.net).

Beginners will learn in swimming pools and sheltered harbours, but for experienced divers the top location is the lava reef off Pasito Blanco, where there are schools of grouper and moray eels.

Parascending, involving flying up to 200m (660ft) in a parachute while attached to a boat, is available at Puerto Rico and Playa del Inglés. This is an expensive thrill, but like many of these activities, it is sometimes available at a discount when combined with a boat trip.

Walks and Tours

1 LAS PALMAS
Walk

This gentle walk explores the old quarter of Las Palmas, with its historic houses, cobbled streets and shady squares. It's an ideal introduction for first-time visitors to the city, with visits to the cathedral, Columbus' house, Casa de Colón, and Museo Canario.

DISTANCE 3km (2 miles) **TIME** 1.5–2 hours
START/END POINT Parque San Telmo ✚ 186 C2

The renovated Pérez Galdos theatre

1–2
Leaving the bus station, walk across **Parque San Telmo** (▶ 62) with the military headquarters in front of you, then turn left along **Calle Mayor de Triana** (▶ 62). This pedestrian shopping street begins close to the small chapel on the south side of the park. Walk along this promenade, admiring the mix of Modernist and neo-classical façades. Continue to the end of the street as it bends round to the left. Turn left to reach **Teatro Pérez Galdós**, the city's principal theatre. First opened in 1858, it burned down in 1918 and was rebuilt and named after the Canarian novelist. Outside the theatre, a bust of the French composer Camille Saint-Saëns recalls his visit to Gran Canaria.

2–3
Take care as you cross the busy highway which separates the district of Triana from Vegueta. Now you are approaching the oldest part of the city. On the

(map showing: Parque San Telmo, BRAVO MURILLO, Guaguas Estación Central de Autobuses, AVENIDA RAFAEL CABRERA, Mayor de Triana, with markers 1 and 10)

far side of the road, look into the **Mercado de Vegueta** (➤ 61) or stop for a coffee and a plate of *churros* (dough fritters) in one of the market bars.

3–4

Exit the Mercado de Vegueta via **Calle Mendizábal**, the main commercial street of Vegueta, lined with cafés and bars. The fine Renaissance building at the end of the street was founded in 1776 as a royal society for "friends of Spain". Outside is a bust of Don José de

Viera y Clavijo (1731–1813), the first historian of the Canary Islands. Turn right along **Calle de los Balcones**, one of the prettiest streets in Las Palmas, with its typical Canarian houses and balconies. Note, on your right, the Casa de la Orden del Cachorro Canario (the Order of the Felt Hat), a society dedicated to Canarian culture. Also on this street is the **Centro Atlántico de Arte Moderno** (➤ 61), a modern art museum hiding behind an 18th-century façade.

4–5

Calle de los Balcones ends behind the cathedral in **Plaza del Pilar Nuevo**, dominated by the Biblioteca Colombina, a beautiful old house containing the library of the Casa de Colón. Turn left here across a leafy square of bougainvillea, laurel and palm trees, then right into Calle Espíritu Santo. The

TAKING A BREAK
Of several pavement cafés on and around Plaza de Cairasco, the best spot is the terrace of the Hotel Madrid (➤ 66).

entrance to the cathedral, **Catedral de Santa Ana** (▶ 56) is a short distance along this street on your right.

5–6

At the next junction, turn left along Calle Reloj and then right along Calle Dr Chil to reach the **Museo Canario** (▶ 52). Now go left along Calle Dr Verneau, passing the museum entrance. Continue on this street for two blocks, then turn right along Calle Rosario into Plaza de Pilar, a peaceful square with an 18th-century fountain at its centre. On Sunday mornings this is the venue for a busy **flower and craft market**, with music, dancing and activities for children. The church of Santo Domingo dates from the 16th century and contains an altarpiece by the Canarian artist Luján Pérez.

6–7

Leave the square in the northwest corner along Calle Pedro Díaz, climbing gently towards Paseo Sor Jesús. Turn right here along the walls of an old hospital and right

Catedral Santa Anna seen across the plaza surrounded by trees and bougainvillea

again along Calle Castillo, where there are several fine old Canarian houses. As you walk down this street, there are good views of the Catedral Santa Ana ahead. The street ends in **Plaza del Espíritu Santo**, one of Vegueta's most charming spaces, with a covered fountain set in its own small garden and a stately palm tree. The chapel here dates from 1615 and has a revered image of Christ, which is used in the city's Good Friday processions. The house next to the church was the home of Silvestre de Balboa, born in Las Palmas in 1563 and author of the first known work of Cuban literature.

7–8

From Plaza del Espíritu Santo it is just a few steps downhill to **Plaza de Santa Ana**, once the city's main square. The square is surrounded by flat-roofed Renaissance mansions containing, among others, the episcopal palace and the residence of the former governors. Bronze dogs, symbols of the Canary Islands, stand guard at the far end of the square. The best place to take it all in is from a vantage point on the steps of the old town hall, facing the Catedral Santa Ana. Turn left in front of the cathedral and take the next right to reach **Plazoleta de los**

Alamos. Directly in front of you as you enter this small square is the façade of the **Casa de Colón** (▶ 59), with its carved stone doorway, wooden balconies, gargoyles and coat of arms. Keep straight on along Calle Colón to reach the entrance to the house.

8–9

Just beyond the Casa de Colón, **Plaza de San Antonio Abad** marks the origins of the city. It was here that Juan Rejón founded the city in 1478 – there's a plaque on the wall in Pasaje Pedro de Algaba. The small chapel here was the first church in Las Palmas, where Columbus is said to have prayed for the success of his voyages to America. Retrace your steps along Calle Colon and turn right down Calle Herrería to return to the highway, built on the site of the Guiniguada ravine. Cross the road to reach **Plaza de las Ranas**, named after the frogs which used to live in the stream. The area around the Galeria de Arte Monopol shopping mall is now a popular night haunt.

9–10

Turn left just beyond the library to reach **Plaza de Cairasco**. This triangular square is perhaps the most emblematic of all Las Palmas' open spaces. At the centre is a fountain and a bust of Bartolomé Cairasco, a 16th-century Canarian poet. To the right is the Hotel Madrid, where Franco spent the night before launching his military rebellion in 1936. The **Gabinete Literario**, dominating the square, is Las Palmas' finest 19th-century building, with neo-classical and Modernist touches. Founded in 1844, it is closed to visitors, but you can peer inside at the sumptuous entrance hall and grand staircase.

Next to the square, **Alameda de Colón** is a stylish promenade with benches and a statue of Columbus (1892). Leave Plaza de Cairasco via Calle Malteses and retrace your steps along Calle Mayor de Triana to Parque San Telmo.

The façade of the Casa de Colón

Right: The monument to Bartolomé Cairasco in his eponymous square

2 CRUZ DE TEJEDA

Walk

DISTANCE 4km (2.5 miles) **TIME** 1–1.5 hours
START/END POINT Cruz de Tejeda ✚ 179 F2

This short walk in the mountains gives truly spectacular views for the minimum of effort. It can easily be incorporated into the drive across the cumbre (▶ 161), or combined with a day-trip to Cruz de Tejeda and a hearty lunch.

1–2

Begin at **Cruz de Tejeda** (▶ 113) with the *parador* behind you and take the cobbled path to the right of Hotel El Refugio (▶ 117). When the path divides, keep to the left fork, climbing between bushes of *retama* (broom) and *tajinaste* (viper's bugloss). The path ascends to a stone wall at the boundary of a fenced-off estate clearly marked with the sign "*Coto privado de ca*" ("No Hunting"). Keep straight ahead, following an **old donkey trail** along a ridge. Take your time admiring the sweeping panorama of the mountains. The landmarks of **Roque Nublo** (▶ 110) and **Roque Bentaiga** (▶ 108) are clearly visible in the foreground, while Mount Teide on

Tenerife appears on the horizon, usually floating on a sea of clouds. This is a wonderful place to watch the sunset.

2–3

Leaving the ridge, the path drops down between fences and pine trees towards a large pair of gates, then continues along a **grit track** between slopes planted with pines. When the track swings round

On clear days Tenerife seems to actually float above the clouds

Native Canarian pines

Becerra, a lookout point on the old pilgrim route from San Mateo to San Bartolomé de Tirajana.

Leaving the *mirador*, return to **Cruz de Tejeda** by the same route. On a clear day the superb views stretch north as far as La Isleta in Las Palmas.

sharply to the left, continue straight ahead by scrambling up on to a **path** where you are immediately rewarded with a magnificent view over the Barranco de la Mina. The houses of **Vega de San Mateo** (➤ 93), way down in the valley, sparkle in the distance.

3–4
The path now drops down to join a tarmac road. Turn right and keep to the road for around 200m (220 yards), walking in the shade of tall Canary pine trees to your left and Canada pines to your right. When you see a **white house** on the right, leave the road to walk up the concrete driveway and follow the path to the left of the house. Keep to your left, and follow this mostly flagstoned path as it winds around the hillside, parallel to and above the road. When the path drops back down to the road, turn right to reach the **Mirador de**

3 COSTA CANARIA
Walk

DISTANCE 8km (5 miles) **TIME** 3 hours
START POINT San Agustín ✚ 184 B2 **END POINT** Faro de Maspalomas ✚ 183 F1

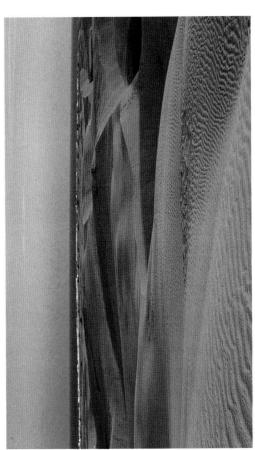

This delightful walk follows the Maspalomas coastline, also known as the Costa Canaria. On foot it is easy to appreciate the varied scenery of this stretch of coast, and the subtly differing character of the various resorts. With good bus connections to the start and finish, it's an easy day trip from any of the south coast resorts. The walk is mostly flat and can be done in good, comfortable sandals – apart from the dunes, which are best crossed barefoot.

1–2
Ask the bus driver to let you off at the **San Agustín** roundabout, then take the short road downhill to the **beach** at San Agustín. Before you begin your walk, follow the beachside promenade around to your left until it runs out. From here you have a good view of the entire walk, with the Faro de Maspalomas

The highlight of this walk is the trek across the Dunas de Maspalomas

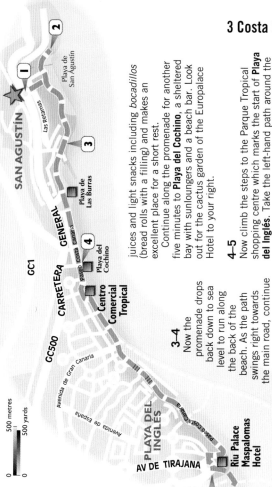

(lighthouse), your ultimate destination, visible beyond the sand dunes.

2–3

Retrace your steps along the **promenade** as it passes behind the beach and alongside the gardens of the Melia Tamarindos Hotel. The wide beach is rarely crowded and in the early morning it can be a very peaceful spot. The path crosses the end of the beach beneath a row of pines and climbs on to a headland where it clings to the rocks between seafront bungalows and a series of rocky coves.

After a few minutes, go round the corner to see the large expanse of **Playa de las Burras** beneath you. This beach of golden sand, between San Agustín and Playa del Inglés, has a name which means "beach of the she-donkeys" in Spanish.

juices and light snacks including *bocadillos* (bread rolls with a filling) and makes an excellent place for a short rest.

Continue along the promenade for another five minutes to **Playa del Cochino**, a sheltered bay with sunloungers and a beach bar. Look out for the cactus garden of the Europalace Hotel to your right.

3–4

Now the promenade drops back to sea level to run along the back of the beach. As the path swings right towards the main road, continue straight ahead to cross the wooden footbridge at the mouth of a small *barranco* (gorge). The bar on the bridge sells freshly squeezed

4–5

Now climb the steps to the Parque Tropical shopping centre which marks the start of **Playa del Inglés**. Take the left-hand path around the shopping centre to rejoin the promenade, now wider and known as the **Paseo Costa Canaria**. Pine and bamboo trees cling to the slopes as you look down over the cliffs, with views of the Maspalomas sand dunes in the distance.

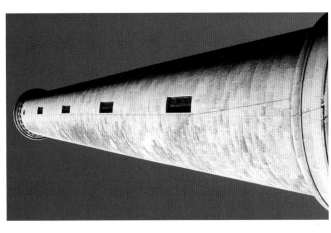

lighthouse. Make sure that you have plenty of water before you set out.

As a rule, it is easier to weave in and out between the dunes than to attempt to take a direct path, as some of the dunes are up to 10m (32 feet) deep. The contours are constantly changing as the sand is sculpted by the wind. With the breeze against your face and hot sand between your toes, this is a real back-to-nature experience.

It's worth noting that there are many nudists sunbathing around here and that this is a popular gay cruising area.

The walk across the **dunes** takes about an hour. Using the lighthouse to guide you, head towards Maspalomas beach, passing behind the lagoon to rejoin the crowds of bathers. Now walk along the beach until you come to the **Faro de Maspalomas** (lighthouse).

Buses to **San Agustín** and **Playa del Inglés** leave just inland from here. Alternatively, if you still have some energy, you can return to Playa del Inglés by walking along the shoreline (allow around 1.5 hours).

The end of the road for this walk is the lighthouse at Maspalomas, which you can use as a beacon to guide your way across the dunes

TAKING A BREAK
There are numerous restaurants, bars and cafés in the **Parque Tropical shopping centre** (▶ 159) and behind the beach in **Playa del Inglés** (▶ 127).

The promenade gets busier as you approach the heart of the resort. Soon you reach a long flight of steps which leads down to the beach. Continue on the promenade that runs high above the beach.

As the beach starts to widen, the path descends a steep staircase, crosses a road and climbs up again on the other side to leave the resort behind. Before long you are walking beside the dunes.

When the path finally runs out, follow the bend around to your right to reach a road, then turn left and walk through the archway of the **Riu Palace Maspalomas Hotel** (▶ 144) to arrive at the viewpoint overlooking the dunes. You can finish your walk here if you prefer not to continue over the dunes.

5–6
Take off your shoes and begin the long and demanding trek across the dunes towards the

4 ACROSS THE CUMBRE

Drive

DISTANCE 130km (80 miles) **TIME** 4 hours
START/END POINT Las Palmas ⊞ 181 E4

This half-day drive across the sierra provides a vivid introduction to the diverse landscapes of the island. As the green, alpine north gives way to the harsh, arid south, it is easy to see why it is known as a continent in miniature.

1–2

Leave **Las Palmas** on the GC110, following signs to Tafira. As you drive out of the city on this busy road, look up to admire the pastel-coloured houses of the *barrios* of **San Roque** and **San Juan**, clinging to the hillsides like some Cubist fantasy. The dual carriageway (divided highway) climbs steeply out of Las Palmas, passing the university and a water treatment plant. Shortly after the **Jardín Canario** (▶ 81), the road narrows to a single lane and runs through Tafira Alta. Continue through **Monte Lentiscal**, where much of Gran Canaria's wine is produced, to **Santa Brígida**. These prosperous villages have virtually become suburbs of Las Palmas, where wealthy

The houses of San Roque add an unexpected splash of colour

Canarios have homes away from the bustle and noise of the city.

2–3

Now the serious climbing begins. The road is shaded by tall pines and eucalyptus trees as it winds up towards **Vega de San Mateo** (▶ 93).

The higher you go, the greener everything becomes. The views are magnificent, but there are many twists and turns and you need to keep your eyes on the road. Eventually you reach **Cruz de Tejeda** (▶ 113), a good place to break your journey, with a restaurant and cafés. If you want to stretch your legs, take the short walk from here to the **Mirador de Becerra** (▶ 113).

3–4

The next section of the route is the most spectacular as you snake down towards the village of **Tejeda** (▶ 114). The monoliths of **Roque Bentaiga** (▶ 108) and **Roque Nublo** (▶ 110) loom dramatically. Continue on the GC60, passing Roque Bentaiga on the way to **Ayacata**, a busy mountain crossroads with several restaurants and bars (▶ 110).

4–5

Drive through Ayacata, ignoring the turn-off to the right. The road now becomes the GC65, signposted to San Bartolomé de Tirajana. There are fine views to your right over the Chira reservoir as you climb to the **Cruz Grande pass** (1,200m/3,937 feet), which forms a natural barrier between north and south. The landscape visibly changes, becoming harsher and more rugged as you gaze down a series

of gorges towards the south coast. Inland, the views are dominated by **Risco Blanco**, a huge wall of white rock.

The road continues to **San Bartolomé de Tirajana** (▶ 114), the small town at the head of the Barranco de Tirajana.

Roque Bentaiga dominates the landscape

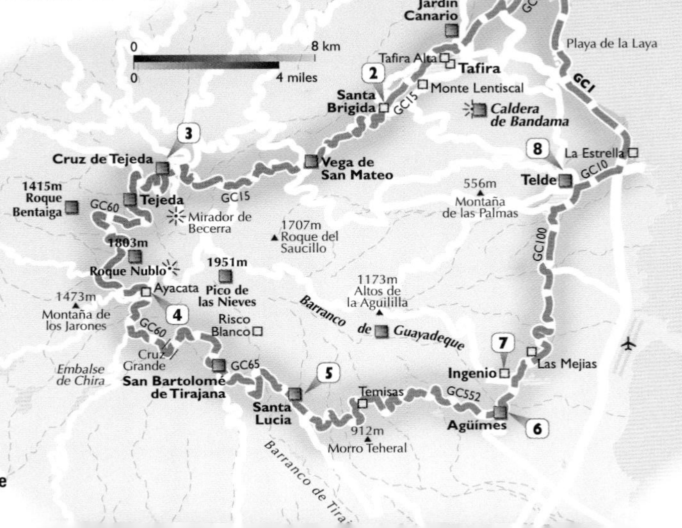

Map labels

LAS PALMAS

San Juan
Playa de la Laya
GC1
GC110
Jardín Canario
Tafira Alta
Tafira
Monte Lentiscal
Santa Brígida
GC15
Caldera de Bandama
La Estrella
GC10
Telde
GC100
556m
Montaña de las Palmas
Vega de San Mateo
Las Mejías
Ingenio
GC52
Agüimes
1173m
Altos de la Aguililla
Barranco de Guayadeque
Temisas
912m
Morro Teheral
1707m
Roque del Saucillo
Mirador de Becerra
GC15
1951m
Pico de las Nieves
Risco Blanco
GC65
Santa Lucía
Barranco de Tira
Cruz de Tejeda
Tejeda
GC60
1803m
Roque Nublo
Ayacata
GC60
Cruz Grande
San Bartolomé de Tirajana
1415m
Roque Bentaiga
1473m
Montaña de los Jarones
Embalse de Chira

0   4 miles
0   8 km

(If you are staying on the south coast, you could complete the tour at this point and drive through the Barranco de Fataga to Playa del Inglés.)

Stay on the GC65 as it passes through San Bartolomé and continue to the village of **Santa Lucía** (➤ 115).

5–6

As you leave Santa Lucía, there is a fork in the road. Take the left fork, signposted to Las Palmas and Agüimes. At first the road climbs through a barren, rocky moonscape, but after 8km (5 miles) the village of **Temisas** appears as a cluster of white houses, surrounded by olive groves and clinging to the steep slopes of a gorge. Now the landscape grows greener once again, with more olive trees and cacti on the hillsides as you descend towards **Agüimes** (➤ 138).

6–7

At the intersection turn left to enter Agüimes, then left again to avoid the town. The road crosses the **Barranco de Guayadeque** (➤ 124). On the far side of the *barranco*, look towards Agüimes to see the houses perched above the ravine. Next is **Ingenio**, a small town known for arts and crafts. At the traffic lights

Take a detour along the Barranco de Guayadeque, where descendants of the original Guanches live in caves not much changed from earlier times

turn right into the one-way system towards a roundabout (traffic circle), where a monument of a sugar press recalls the town's history of sugar production. Take the last exit from the roundabout to head back up the hill into Ingenio.

7–8

Reaching a crossroads, turn right onto the GC100, following signs to Telde. The road passes the northern suburb of **Las Mejías** (which is home to a handicrafts museum ➤ 126) and crosses a rocky plateau with views of Gando Airport before descending to **Telde** (➤ 92). On entering Telde, turn right onto the ring road and follow signs to **Las Palmas** to return via the coastal motorway.

TAKING A BREAK

For lunch try El Refugio (➤ 117) or Hao at Santa Lucía (➤ 117) or La Hacienda de Molino (➤ 117).

5 AROUND THE ISLAND

Drive

DISTANCE 190km (118 miles) **TIME** 1 day
START/END POINT Puerto de Mogán ⊞ 182 B3

This one-day drive follows the shoreline before heading inland into a fertile valley. It may seem a lot of ground to cover, but because of the fast motorways along the north and east coasts, it is possible. Along the way are all the different sides of Gran Canaria: mega-resorts, fishing villages and banana plantations as well as a testing but dramatic stretch of coastal corniche.

1–2

Begin in **Puerto de Mogán** (▶ 136) and head inland along the valley towards Mogán. After just over 1km (0.5 miles), turn right to join the GC500 coast road to Las Palmas. From here to Puerto Rico the road hugs the cliffs, passing a succession of bays and inlets which are slowly being taken over by tourism.

Shortly after the beach at **Playa de los Amadores** (▶ 141), you round a bend to see the apartment blocks of **Puerto Rico** (▶ 141) climbing up the steep hillsides in front of you.

2–3

Continue on the coast road heading towards **Arguineguín** (▶ 139). When yhou are just beyond Arguineguin, bear right to stay on the GC500. Passing a large banana plantation, turn right at the roundabout (traffic circle) to

Masts and sails line up against the jetty in the exclusive private marina of Pasito Blanco

climb on to a headland overlooking a cement factory. Between here and Maspalomas there are numerous small beaches and coves. During the week this area is usually pretty much deserted and you can have an entire beach to yourself.

All this may change as this coastline is earmarked for further development, with new roads, golf-courses and tourist villages stretching all the way from Maspalomas to Mogán. The yacht marina at **Pasito Blanco**, up until now an exclusive spot, is planned to be connected to Maspalomas and the dunes by a seafront promenade.

3–4

Shortly after passing **Las Meloneras**, the road crests a hill and the conurbation of Playa del Inglés and Maspalomas is spread out beneath you. During the day, the **Dunas de Maspalomas** (▶ 130) are visible to your right; at night, the lights of **Playa del Inglés** (▶ 127) sparkle

6–7

You have now exchanged one motorway for another as you find yourself on the main road running along the north coast. As you emerge from the tunnel, look out for the **Auditorio Alfredo Kraus** to your right (▶71) behind the Las Arenas shopping centre at the end of **Playa de las Canteras** (▶65). The road now follows the coastline through a succession of small villages.

7–8

Just after **El Pagador**, where white houses jut out on a spit, the road climbs sharply to the **Puente da Silva**, a huge bridge high above a gorge. After more bridges and tunnels, the volcanic pyramid at **Gáldar** comes into view (▶95).

Keep on the GC2 as it bypasses Gáldar towards **Agaete** (▶88). When the motorway runs out, turn right and head to **Puerto de las Nieves** (▶90). This is a good place to break your journey with a seafood lunch on the beach.

8–9

Take the road from Puerto de las Nieves to Agaete then turn right following signs to **San Nicolás de Tolentino** (▶142). Although it is

below. Continue on the GC500 as it passes through this area, skirting Playa del Inglés on its way to the neighbouring resort of **San Agustín** (▶120).

4–5

The road now hugs the coastline again on its way to **Juan Grande**. This ordinary-looking village is the ancestral home of the Vega Grande family, responsible for much of the tourist development along the south coast. Just beyond Juan Grande, when the windmills of **Pozo Izquierdo** appear to your right, leave the GC500 to join the GC1 motorway to Las Palmas.

5–6

The motorway now passes factories, shopping malls and Gando Airport on its way to Las Palmas. After bypassing **Telde**, it returns to the coast and as you round a bend **Playa de la Laja** comes into view. Now you are approaching the southern outskirts of Las Palmas.

As you enter the city, the motorway becomes the Avenida Marítima, bordered by a waterfront promenade popular with walkers and cyclists. Passing the yacht club, follow signs to Agaete and go through a tunnel to join the GC2.

The windmills of Pozo Izquierdo

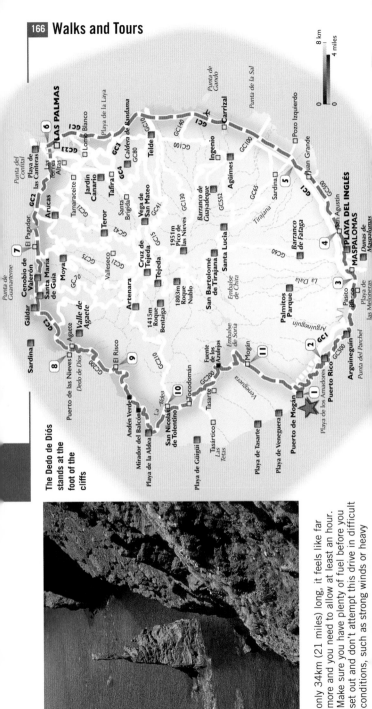

The Dedo de Diós stands at the foot of the cliffs

only 34km (21 miles) long, it feels like far more and you need to allow at least an hour. Make sure you have plenty of fuel before you set out and don't attempt this drive in difficult conditions, such as strong winds or heavy

The road from San Nicolas de Tolentino running up to one of the reservoirs, with volcanic peaks visible in the background

rain. The road climbs steeply into the hills and then sweeps around a gorge with views back down over Puerto de las Nieves and the **Dedo de Dios** (Finger of God) rock (▶ 90). The landscape here is very stark. Nothing grows on the hillsides except spiky bushes of *cardón* (euphorbia).

After passing a rocky outcrop, the road swings left, leaving the gorge behind. The cliffs drop sheer into the ocean beneath you. Eventually the road turns inland to reach the isolated settlement of **El Risco**, where a valley bed planted with gardens leads down to a remote and beautiful beach.

9–10

The views grow ever more dramatic as you approach the **Andén Verde** (▶ 90) coastal corniche, with Tenerife visible across the water and layer upon layer of volcanic cliffs receding into the distance.

As the road begins its slow descent into the plain of San Nicolás, pull into the well-marked parking area at the **Mirador del Balcón** to take in the views along the coast. The road now winds down the hillsides to the mouth of the **Barranco de la Aldea**. A short detour at this point leads to **Puerto de la Aldea** (▶ 142), with its shingle beach, harbour and promenade.

Leaving the port, follow the GC200 inland to the dusty town of **San Nicolás de Tolentino**, with the striking silhouette of **Roque Nublo** (▶ 110) visible on the skyline.

10–11

Reaching San Nicolás, turn right before a small windmill, following signs to **Mogán** (▶136). You are now heading inland, on a good road with numerous hairpin bends. **Tocodomán**, with the **Cactualdea Cactus Park** (▶142), makes a pleasant diversion and

offers a chance to stretch your legs.
The GC200 continues to climb into the foothills of the sierra. Signposts point the way down a series of valleys, to the remote west coast beaches of **Tasartico, Tasarte** and **Veneguera** (▶141). Roadside cafés advertise fresh papaya juice.

Shortly after the turn-off for Tasarte, you reach **Fuente de los Azulejos**, a remarkable multicoloured rock formation named after its resemblance to Portuguese tiles. It's worth getting out of the car here for a close-up look at this geological oddity. Passing the road to Veneguera and a turn-off leading to the high sierra (strictly for adventurous drivers!), the GC200 now drops down to Mogán.

Follow the road through the town centre and continue along a fertile, well-populated valley to return to **Puerto de Mogán**, where you can have a cooling drink after a long day's drive in one of the harbour cafés.

TAKING A BREAK

Try Las Nasas at Puerto de las Nieves (▶98), a good seafood restaurant, or one of the many seafood places at Puerto de la Aldea.

Unwind after your long drive with a stroll around the marina at Puerto de Mogán and check out some of the yachts

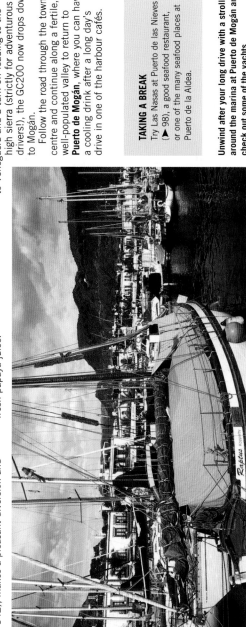

Practicalities

BEFORE YOU GO

WHAT YOU NEED

		UK	Germany	USA	Canada	Australia	Ireland	Netherlands	Spain
● Required / ○ Suggested / ▲ Not required / △ Not applicable	Some countries require a passport to remain valid for a minimum period (usually at least six months) beyond the date of entry – check beforehand.								
Passport/National Identity Card		●	●	●	●	●	●	●	▲
Visa		▲	▲	▲	▲	▲	▲	▲	▲
Onward or Return Ticket		○	○	●	●	●	○	○	○
Health Inoculations (tetanus and polio)		▲	▲	▲	▲	▲	▲	▲	▲
Health Documentation (▶ 174, Health)		●	●	▲	▲	▲	●	●	▲
Travel Insurance		○	○	○	○	○	○	○	○
Driving Licence (national)		●	●	●	●	●	●	●	●
Car Insurance Certificate		●	●	●	●	●	●	●	○
Car Registration Document		●	●	●	●	●	●	●	○

WHEN TO GO

Gran Canaria

Low season   High season

JAN	FEB	MAR	APR	MAY	JUN	JUL	AUG	SEP	OCT	NOV	DEC
22°C	23°C	26°C	22°C	25°C	26°C	26°C	28°C	26°C	26°C	24°C	23°C
72°F	73°F	79°F	72°F	77°F	79°F	79°F	82°F	79°F	79°F	75°F	73°F

☀ Sun   ☁ Cloud   🌧 Wet   ⛅ Sun/Showers

The temperatures above are the average daily maximum for each month. Minimum temperatures rarely drop below 15°C (59°F); there is a year-round spring climate. On the south coast, which has over 300 days of sunshine a year, summer temperatures often exceed 30°C (80°F). The sea temperature varies from 19°C (66°F) in January to 24°C (75°F) in September. Most of the rain falls in the north, and there is occasional snow in the central mountains. The north is also affected by the *mar de nubes* "sea of clouds", low-lying clouds brought by the trade winds, and the *panza de burro* "donkey's belly", a grey haze which produces intense heat in summer. There is a second peak in July and August, when many Spanish families are on holiday. The quietest months are May, June, September and October.

GETTING ADVANCE INFORMATION

WEBSITES

■ Spanish Tourist Board:
www.spain.info
www.tourspain.co.uk
■ Gran Canaria Info:
www.turismodecanarias.
com

■ Gran Canaria Tourist Board:
www.grancanaria.com
■ Maspalomas Costa Canaria:
www.maspalomas-tonight.
com

In the UK

Spanish National
Tourist Office
79 New Cavendish Street
(by appiontment only)
London W1W 6XB
☎ 020 7486 8077

GETTING THERE

By Air There are numerous charter flights to Las Palmas throughout the year from London and other European cities. Most seats are sold by tour operators as part of a package holiday, but it is usually possible to buy a flight-only deal through travel agents or on the internet. For independent travellers, the disadvantage of charter flights is that you are usually restricted to periods of 7 or 14 days.

The Spanish national airline, **Iberia**, has regular scheduled flights to Las Palmas via Madrid and Barcelona, with connections to major cities worldwide. From the USA, Canada, Australia and New Zealand, it is often cheaper to fly to London or Amsterdam and pick up a charter flight from there. Flight times are approximately four hours from London and two hours from Madrid.

By Sea The ferry company **Trasmediterránea** has a weekly car ferry service from Cádiz on the Spanish mainland to Tenerife and Gran Canaria. The journey from Cádiz to Las Palmas takes around 50 hours.

Inter-island Travel Binter Canarias has daily flights from Las Palmas to Tenerife and the other Canary islands. There are also regular ferry services from Las Palmas to ports in Fuerteventura, Lanzarote and Tenerife with connections to the other islands.

A high-speed jetfoil connects Las Palmas several times daily with Santa Cruz de Tenerife. The **Fred Olsen** line has up to eight ferries a day from Puerto de las Nieves to Santa Cruz de Tenerife, with a journey time of one hour.

TIME

 Unlike the rest of Spain, the Canary Islands observe Greenwich Mean Time (GMT). Summer time (GMT+1) operates from the last Sunday in March to the last Sunday in October.

CURRENCY AND FOREIGN EXCHANGE

Currency On 1 January 2002, the Euro replaced the peseta as the official currency of Spain. Euro coins and notes are also legal tender in many other European countries, including France, Germany, Italy and Ireland. Euro notes come in denominations of 5, 10, 20, 50, 100, 200 and 500; coins come in denominations of 1, 2, 5, 10, 20 and 50 cents.

Credit cards Major credit cards are widely accepted.

Exchange Banks generally offer the best rates for changing foreign currency and travellers' cheques, though money can also be changed at many travel agents, exchange bureaux and hotels. When changing travellers' cheques, you will need to show your passport. You can also withdraw cash from ATM (cashpoint) machines using your credit or debit card and a PIN (personal identification number). Your own bank will usually make a charge for this service.

WHEN YOU ARE THERE

CLOTHING SIZES

UK	Rest of Europe	USA	
36	46	36	
38	48	38	
40	50	40	
42	52	42	Suits
44	54	44	
46	56	46	
7	41	8	
7.5	42	8.5	
8.5	43	9.5	
9.5	44	10.5	Shoes
10.5	45	11.5	
11	46	12	
14.5	37	14.5	
15	38	15	
15.5	39/40	15.5	
16	41	16	Shirts
16.5	42	16.5	
17	43	17	
8	34	6	
10	36	8	
12	38	10	
14	40	12	Dresses
16	42	14	
18	44	16	
4.5	38	6	
5	38	6.5	
5.5	39	7	
6	39	7.5	Shoes
6.5	40	8	
7	41	8.5	

NATIONAL HOLIDAYS

1 Jan	New Year's Day
6 Jan	Epiphany
19 Mar	St Joseph's Day
Mar/Apr	Good Friday, Easter Monday
1 May	Labour Day
30 May	Canary Islands' Day
May/June	Corpus Christi
15 Aug	Assumption of the Virgin
12 Oct	Spanish National Day
1 Nov	All Saints' Day
6 Dec	Constitution Day
8 Dec	Feast of the Immaculate Conception
25 Dec	Christmas Day

OPENING HOURS

○ Shops   ● Post Offices
● Offices ○ Museums
● Banks   ○ Pharmacies

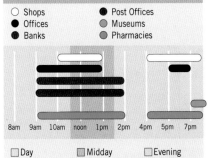

8am 9am 10am noon 1pm 2pm 4pm 5pm 7pm

☐ Day   ☐ Midday   ☐ Evening

Shops The larger department stores in Las Palmas and many shops in the resorts stay open throughout the day. Most shops are closed on Sundays.
Banks Banks are closed on Sundays.
Restaurants Many restaurants in the larger resorts are open daily from around 10am to midnight.
Museums and attractions Hours vary. As a general guideline they are open 10–1 and 4–8, but it is best to consult the individual times given for each sight in this guide.

TIME DIFFERENCES

GMT
12 noon

Gran Canaria
12 noon

mainland Spain
1 pm

Germany
1 pm

USA (NY)
7 am

PERSONAL SAFETY

Violence against tourists is unusual. Theft from cars is the most common form of crime, particularly in Las Palmas.

- Do not leave valuables on the beach or poolside.
- Always lock valuables in hotel safety deposit boxes.
- Never leave anything inside your car.
- Avoid the seamier streets in the port area of Las Palmas at night.

Police assistance:
☎ **112** from any phone

TELEPHONES

There are public telephones on almost every street corner, with instructions in several languages. Most take coins, credit cards or phonecards (*tarjetas telefónicas*) which are available from post offices, kiosks and shops.

The cheap rate for international calls applies 10pm–8am and all day Sunday.

International Dialling Codes
Dial 00 followed by

UK:	44
USA/Canada:	1
Ireland:	353
Australia:	61
Germany:	49

POST

Post boxes are yellow. The main post office in Las Palmas is at Avenida Primero de Mayo 62. Stamps (*sellos*) are available from post offices, hotels, news kiosks and tobacconists. A postcard to the UK or North Europe will usually take about a week to arrive; allow 10–14 days to the USA.

ELECTRICITY

The power supply is 220 volts. Sockets take continental-style plugs with two round pins. Visitors from the UK will require an adaptor (often available at the airport) and visitors from the USA will require a voltage transformer.

TIPS/GRATUITIES

Tipping is not expected for all services, and rates are lower than in some countries. As a general guide:

Restaurants	10%
Cafés/bars	Discretion
Tour guides	Discretion
Taxis	10%
Hairdressers	10%
Chambermaids	10%
Porters	10%
Lavatories	Discretion

POLICE	112
FIRE	112
AMBULANCE	112

HEALTH

 Insurance Citizens of the European Union and certain other countries receive free medical treatment in Spain with the relevant documentation (EHIC card for UK nationals), although private medical insurance is still advised and is essential for all other visitors.

 Dental Services Dental treatment has to be paid for by all visitors but is usually covered by private medical insurance.

 Weather Visitors from cooler countries are especially vulnerable to the effects of the sun. You should cover up with a high-factor sunblock and drink plenty of non-alcoholic fluids. Children need to be well protected, especially when playing near the sea, as water and sand reflect the sun's rays.

 Drugs Prescription and non-prescription drugs and medicines are available from pharmacies, usually distinguished by a large green cross. Outside normal hours, a notice on the door of each pharmacy should give the address of the nearest duty pharmacist.

 Safe Water Tap water is generally safe to drink but has a high salt content. Mineral water is widely available and cheap, especially when bought at supermarkets in 5-litre (1.3-gallon) containers.

CONCESSIONS

Students Gran Canaria and the other Canary Islands do not attract backpacking youngsters in the same way as other holiday islands and there are few student or youth concessions available. There are no youth hostels and only two official campsites on the island.

Senior Citizens Gran Canaria is an excellent destination for older travellers, especially in winter when the climate is clement. Some hotels and apartments offer long-stay discounts. The best deals are available through tour operators who specialise in holidays for senior citizens.

TRAVELLING WITH A DISABILITY

All new buildings in Spain must have wheelchair access, but many older hotels, apartment blocks and public buildings are still inaccessible. Some buses have doors which lower to ground level for wheelchair access. Before booking discuss your needs with your tour operator or hotel, or go online at www.solmobility.com.

CHILDREN

Hotels and restaurants are generally very child friendly, and many hotels have playgrounds, parks, mini-golf and children's pools. Some tour operators also provide children's clubs and activities as part of your holiday. However, facilities such as baby-changing rooms are rare.

LAVATORIES

There are public lavatories in shopping centres and at some larger beaches. Other useful standbys are department stores, museums and bars.

CUSTOMS

The import of wildlife souvenirs sourced from rare or endangered species may be either illegal or require a special permit. Before buying, check your home country's customs regulations.

CONSULATES AND EMBASSIES

UK	USA	Ireland	Germany	France
☎ 928/ 262-508	☎ 928/ 222-552	☎ 928/ 297-728	☎ 928/ 491-880	☎ 928/ 292-371

SURVIVAL PHRASES

Yes/no **Sí/no**
Please **Por favor**
Thank you **Gracias**
You're welcome **De nada**
Hello **Hola**
Goodbye **Adiós**
Good morning **Buenos días**
Good afternoon **Buenas tardes**
Good night **Buenas noches**
How are you? **¿Qué tal?**
How much is this? **¿Cuánto vale?**
I'm sorry **Lo siento**
Excuse me **Perdone**
I'd like **Me gustaría...**
Open **Abierto**
Closed **Cerrado**

Today **Hoy**
Tomorrow **Mañana**
Yesterday **Ayer**
Monday **Lunes**
Tuesday **Martes**
Wednesday **Miércoles**
Thursday **Jueves**
Friday **Viernes**
Saturday **Sábado**
Sunday **Domingo**

IF YOU NEED HELP

Help! **¡Socorro! / ¡Ayuda!**
Could you help me, please
 ¿Podría ayudarme, por favor?
Do you speak English? **¿Habla inglés?**
I don't understand **No comprendo**
I don't speak Spanish
 No hablo español
Could you call a doctor?
 ¿Podría llamar a un médico, por favor?

DIRECTIONS

I'm lost **Me he perdido**
Where is...? **¿Dónde está?**
How do I get to...?
 ¿Cómo se va...?
the bank **al banco**
the post office
 a la oficina de correos
the train station
 a la estación de trenes
Where are the lavatories?
 ¿Dónde están los servicios?
Left **a la izquierda**
Right **a la derecha**
Straight on **todo recto**
At the corner **en la esquina**
At the traffic-light **en el semáforo**
At the crossroads **en la intersección**

ACCOMMODATION

Do you have a single/double room?
 ¿Le queda alguna habitación
individual/doble?
 with/without bath/WC/shower
 con/sin baño propio/
 lavabo propio/ducha propia
Does that include breakfast?
 ¿Incluye desayuno?
Could I see the room?
 ¿Puedo ver la habitación?
I'll take this room
 Me quedo con esta habitación
The key to room..., please
 La llave de la habitación...,
 por favor
Thank you for your hospitality
 Muchas gracias por la
 hospitalidad

NUMBERS

1 **uno**	11 **once**	21 **veintiuno**	200 **doscientos**
2 **dos**	12 **doce**	22 **veintidós**	300 **trescientos**
3 **tres**	13 **trece**	30 **treinta**	400 **cuatrocientos**
4 **cuatro**	14 **catorce**	40 **cuarenta**	500 **quinientos**
5 **cinco**	15 **quince**	50 **cincuenta**	600 **seiscientos**
6 **seis**	16 **dieciséis**	60 **sesenta**	700 **setecientos**
7 **siete**	17 **diecisiete**	70 **setenta**	800 ochocientos
8 **ocho**	18 **dieciocho**	80 **ochenta**	900 novecientos
9 **nueve**	19 **diecinueve**	90 **noventa**	1000 **mil**
10 **diez**	20 **veinte**	100 **cien**	

RESTAURANT

I'd like to book a table
¿Me gustaría reservar una mesa?
Have you got a table for two, please
¿Tienen una mesa para dos personas, por favor?
Could we see the menu, please?
¿Nos podría traer la carta, por favor?
Could I have the bill, please?
¿La cuenta, por favor?
service charge included
servicio incluido

breakfast **el desayuno**
lunch **el almuerzo**
dinner **la cena**
table **una mesa**
waiter/waitress **camarero/camarera**
starters **los entremeses**
main course **el plato principal**
dessert **postres**
dish of the day **plato del día**
bill **la cuenta**

MENU READER

aceituna olive
ajo garlic
alcachofa artichoke
almejas clams
almendras almonds
anguila eel
arroz rice
atún/bonito tuna

bacalao cod
berenjena aubergine (eggplant)
biftec steak
bocadillo sandwich
boquerones anchovies

calamares squid
caldo broth
callos tripe
cangrejo crab
cebolla onion
cerdo pork
cerezas cherries
cerveza beer
champiñones mushrooms
chorizo spicy sausage
chuleta chop
churros fritters
ciruela plum
cochinillo asado roast suckling pig
codorniz quail
conejo rabbit
cordero lamb
crema cream

criadillas sweetbreads
crudo raw

endibia chicory
ensalada (mixta) mixed salad
ensaladilla rusa Russian salad
espárragos asparagus
espinaca spinach

fideos noodles
filete fillet
flan crème caramel
frambuesa raspberry
fresa strawberry
fruta (de temporade) seasonal fruit
galleta biscuit (cookie)
gambas prawns
garbanzos chickpeas
gazpacho andaluz gazpacho (cold soup)
grosellas red/black currants
guisantes peas

habas broad beans
helado ice-cream
hígado de oca goose liver
huevos fritos/ revueltos fried/scrambled eggs

jamón ham
judías verdes French beans
jugo fruit juice

langosta lobster
langostino crayfish
leche milk
lechuga lettuce
legumbres vegetables
lengua tongue
lenguado sole
liebre hare
lomo de cerdo pork tenderloin

manzana apple
mariscos seafood
mejillones mussels
melocotón peach
melón melon
merluza hake
mero sea bass
morcilla black pudding

pan bread
pato duck
pepino cucumber
pepinillos gherkins
pera pear
perdiz partridge
perejil parsely
pescado fish
pez espada swordfish
pimientos red/ green peppers
piña pineapple

plátano banana
pollo chicken
puerro leek
pulpo octopus

queso cheese

rape monkfish
riñones kidneys
rodaballo turbot

salchicha sausage
salchichón salami
salmón salmon
salmonete red mullet
solomillo de buey fillet of beef
sopa soup

tocino bacon
tortilla española Spanish omelette
tortilla francesa plain omelette
trucha trout

verduras green vegetables

zanahorias carrots

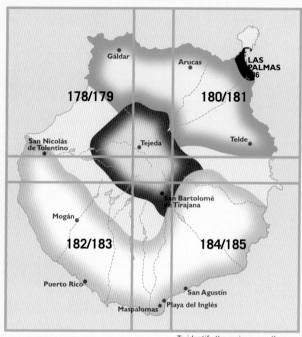

To identify the regions, see the map
on the inside of the front cover

Regional Maps

▬▬▬	Major route	▫	City
▭▭▭	Motorway	▫	Town/village
▬▬▬	Main road	※	Viewpoint/mirador
——	Secondary road	✈	Airport
	Seasonal river	▣	Featured place of interest
▨	National Park		
▨	Built up area		

178–185 0 ———— 3 km
0 ———— 2 miles

Streetplan

▭▭▭	Motorway	ⓘ	Tourist information
▭▭▭	Main road	▣	Featured place of interest
▭▭▭	Minor road		
▨	Important building		
▨	Park/garden		

186 0 ———— 500 metres
0 ———— 500 yards

Atlas

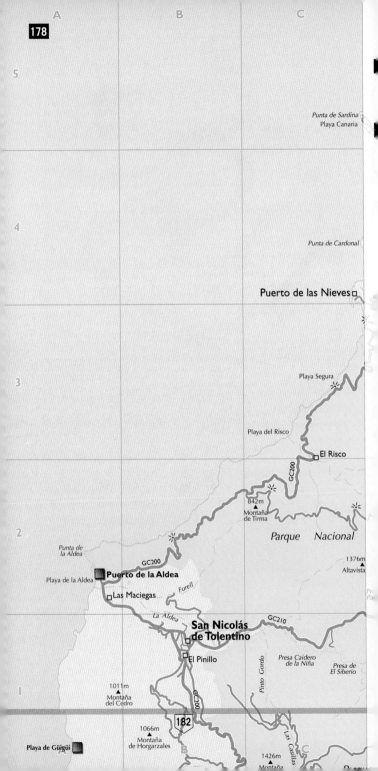

5

A   B   C

Punta de Sardina
Playa Canaria

4

Punta de Cardonal

Puerto de las Nieves □

3

Playa Segura

Playa del Risco

El Risco □

GC200

842m
▲
Montaña
de Tirma

Parque   Nacional

2

Punta de
la Aldea

GC200

1376m
▲
Altavista

Puerto de la Aldea ■

Playa de la Aldea

□ Las Maciegas

Furell

La Aldea

**San Nicolás
de Tolentino**

GC210

□ El Pinillo

Presa Caidero
de la Niña

Presa de
El Siberio

Pinto Gordo

1011m
▲
Montaña
del Cedro

GC200

1

182

1066m
▲
Montaña
de Horgarzales

Playa de Güigüí ■

B

1426m
▲
Montaña

Las Casillas

C

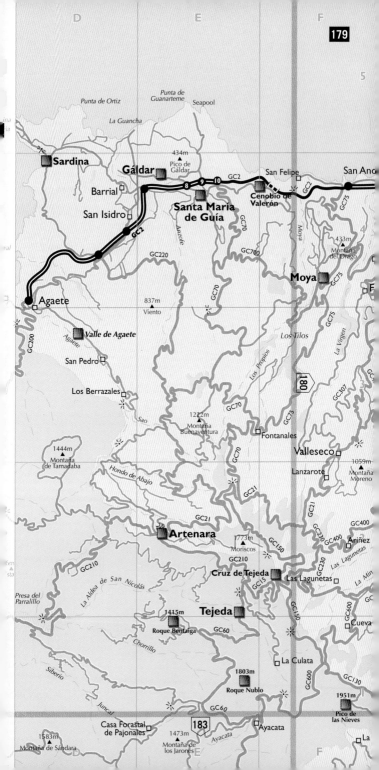

D E F

5

Punta de Ortiz
Punta de Guanarteme
Seapool
La Guancha

Sardina

Gáldar

434m
Pico de Gáldar

San Felipe

San Ano

GC2

Barrial

8 9 10

Cenobio de Valerón

San Isidro

Santa María de Guía

GC2

GC70

Anzofe

Moya

GC700

GC220

GC70

433m
Montaña del Drago

Moya

GC75

F

Agaete

837m
Viento

GC200

Valle de Agaete

Agaete

San Pedro

Los Tilos

Los Propios

La Virgen

180

Los Berrazales

Sao

1222m
Montaña Buenaventura

GC70

GC75

GC307

Valleseco

1444m
Montaña de Tamadaba

Hondo de Abajo

1059m
Montaña Moreno

Fontanales

Lanzarote

GC70

GC21

GC21

GC400

GC21

Presa del Parralillo

GC210

La Aldea de San Nicolás

Artenara

1773m
Moriscos

GC210

GC230

GC400

Ariñez

Las Lagunetas

GC230

GC150

Cruz de Tejeda

GC15

Las Lagunetas

La Min

1415m
Roque Bentaiga

Tejeda

GC60

GC150

Cueva

Chorrillo

Siberio

La Culata

GC600

GC

1803m
Roque Nublo

GC130

1951m
Pico de las Nieves

Juncal

GC60

183

Casa Forestal de Pajonales

1473m
Montaña de los Jarones

Ayacata

Ayacata

1583m
Montaña de Sándara

La

E

F

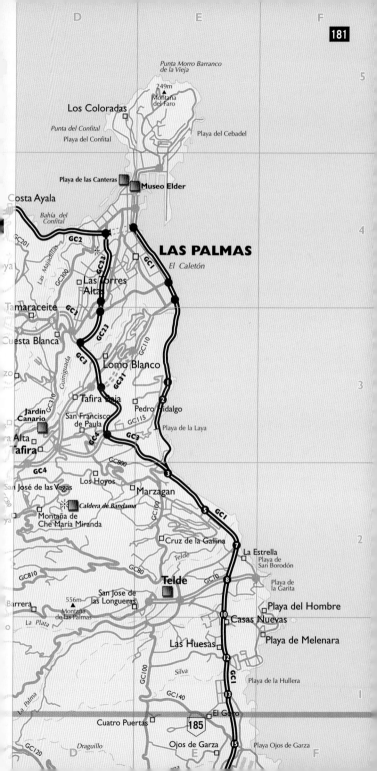

Punta Morro Barranco
de la Vieja

249m
▲ Montaña
del Faro

Los Coloradas

Punta del Confital

Playa del Confital

Playa del Cebadel

Playa de las Canteras

Museo Elder

Costa Ayala

Bahía del
Confital

GC201

GC2

LAS PALMAS

El Caletón

GC1

GC3

Las Majaditas

GC300

**Las Torres
Alta**

Tamaraceite

GC3

GC23

Cuesta Blanca

GC3

Lomo Blanco

GC110

zo

GC31

GC310

Guiniguada

Tafira Baja

Pedro Hidalgo

1

2

**Jardín
Canario**

San Francisco
de Paula

GC115

Playa de la Laya

a Alta

Tafira

GC4

GC3

GC800

GC4

3

GC100

San José de las Vegas

Los Hoyos

✳ **Caldera de Bandama**

Marzagan

5 **GC1**

Montaña de
Che María Miranda

ya

Cruz de la Gallina

7

La Estrella
Playa de
San Borodón

Telde

GC80

8

Playa de
la Garita

GC810

**San José de
las Longueras**

GC10

Playa de
la Garita

Barrera

556m
▲ Montaña
de las Palmas

Telde

10 **Casas Nuevas**

Playa del Hombre

La Plata

Playa de Melenara

o

Las Huesas

12

GC100

Silva

GC1

Playa de la Hullera

La Palma

GC140

13

GC120

Draguillo

Cuatro Puertas

El Goro

185

15

Ojos de Garza

Playa Ojos de Garza

E

F

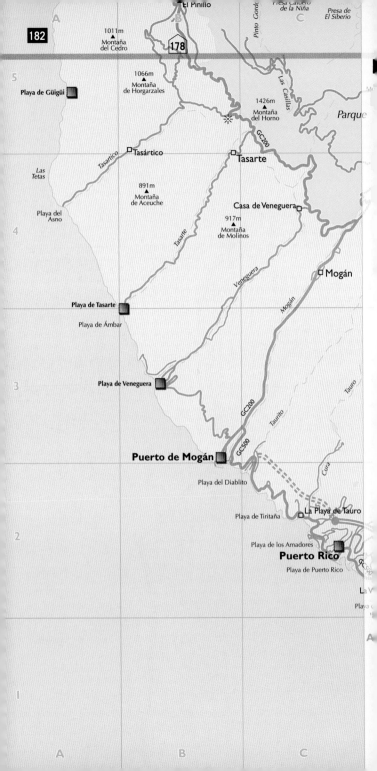

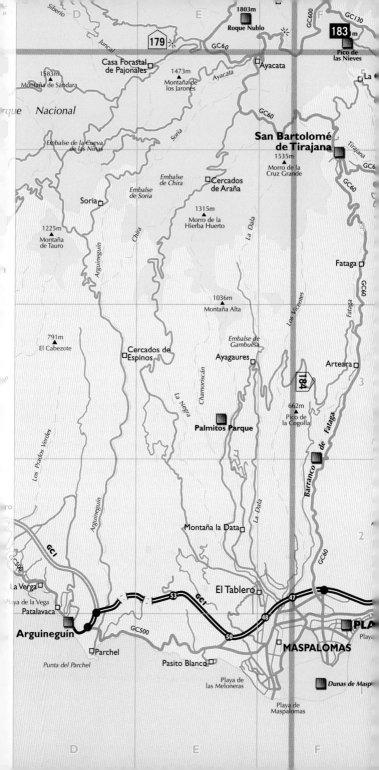

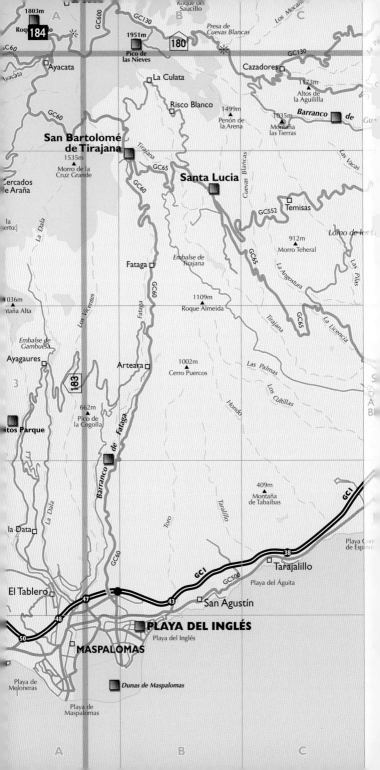

1803m
Roq...

184

GC600

GC130

Roque del Saucillo

Presa de Cuevas Blancas

180

GC130

Los Moca...

A

B

C

1951m
Pico de las Nieves

Cazadores

1173m
Altos de la Aguililla

Ayacata

Ayacata

La Culata

Risco Blanco

1499m
Penón de la Arena

1035m
Montaña las Tierras

Barranco de

Gu...

GC60

San Bartolomé de Tirajana

1535m
Morro de la Cruz Grande

Tirajana

GC65

Santa Lucía

Cuevas Blancas

Las Vacas

Cercados de Araña

la ...erto...

La Dala

GC60

GC552

Temisas

Lomo de los L...

912m
Morro Teheral

GC65

Las Pilas

Fataga

Embalse de Tirajana

La Angostura

1036m
...ntaña Alta

Los Vicentes

GC60

1109m
Roque Almeida

Tirajana

GC65

La Licencia

Embalse de Gambuesa

Ayagaures

183

Arteara

Fataga

1002m
Cerro Puercos

Las Palmas

Los Cutillas

662m
Pico de la Cogolla

Hondo

...tos Parque

La Dala

Barranco de Fataga

409m
Montaña de Tabaibas

GC1

la Data

Toro

Taralillo

38

Playa Corr de Espino...

Playa del Águita

GC1

GC500

Tarajalillo

El Tablero

47

43

San Agustín

48

PLAYA DEL INGLÉS

50

Playa del Inglés

MASPALOMAS

Playa de Meloneras

Dunas de Maspalomas

Playa de Maspalomas

A

B

C

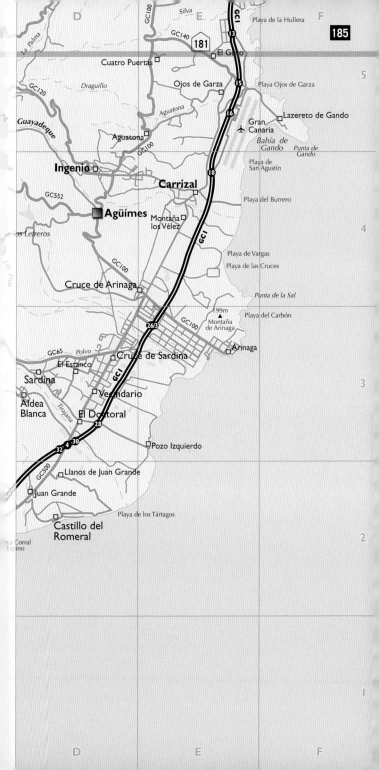

Playa de la Hullera

GC1

Silva

GC140

181

13

El Goro

Cuatro Puertas

GC120

Draguillo

Ojos de Garza

15

Playa Ojos de Garza

Aguatona

16

Lazereto de Gando

Guayadeque

Aguatona

GC100

Gran
Canaria

Bahía de
Gando

Punta de
Gando

Ingenio

18

Playa de
San Agustín

GC552

Carrizal

Agüimes

Montaña
los Vélez

GC1

Playa del Burrero

os Letreros

GC100

Playa de Vargas

Las Pilas

Playa de las Cruces

Cruce de Arinaga

Punta de la Sal

199m
Montaña
de Arinaga

Playa del Carbón

GC100

26 3

Arinaga

GC65

Polvo

El Estanco

Cruce de Sardina

Sardina

GC1

Aldea
Blanca

Vecindario

Tirajana

El Doctoral

28

32 4 30

Pozo Izquierdo

GC500

Llanos de Juan Grande

Juan Grande

Playa de los Tártagos

Castillo del
Romeral

ya Corral
Espino

Picture credits

The Automobile Association would like to thank the following photographers, companies and picture libraries for their assistance in the preparation of this book.

Abbreviations for the picture credits are as follows: (t) top; (b) bottom; (l) left; (r) right; (c) centre; (AA) AA World Travel Library.

2(i) AA/C Sawyer; 2(ii) AA/J Tims; 2(iii) AA/P Bennett; 2(iv) AA/C Sawyer; 3(i) The Travel Library; 3(ii) © PCL/Alamy; 3(iii) © Medio Images/ImageState; 5l AA/C Sawyer; 5r © PCL/Alamy; 6/7 AA/J Tims; 7 AA/J Tims; 8 AA/C Sawyer; 9t © Topham Picturepoint TopFoto. co.uk; 9b AA/P Bennett; 10t AA; 10b © 4Corners Images; 11t AA; 11b Illustrated London News; 12 AA/C Sawyer; 13 AA/C Sawyer; 14 AA/J Tims; 15 AA/J Tims; 16tcl Photolibrary Group; 16cl © Nicholas Pitt/Alamy; 16bl © Eddie Gerald/Alamy; 17tr © Imagebroker/Alamy; 17ctr © Maximilian Weinzierl/Alamy; 17cbr Photolibrary Group; 17br Corbis; 19 © 4 Corners Images; 20 AA/C Sawyer; 21 AA/P Bennett; 22 AA/M Jourdan; 23c AA/C Sawyer; 23b AA/J Tims; 24r © World Pictures/Alamy; 24l AA/N Sumner; 25r AA/C Sawyer; 25l AA/J Tims; 26 Photolibrary Group; 27t © Specialpictures.nl/Alamy; 27c © Westend 61/Alamy; 28 © M. Timothy O'Keefe/ Alamy; 28/29 AA/J Tims; 29 AA/J Tims; 30/31 © ALANDAWSONPHOTOGRAPHY/Alamy; 31 © Islandstock/Alamy; 32 © Maximilian Weinzierl/Alamy; 33t AA/P Bennett; 33b AA/C Sawyer; 34t AA/P Bennett; 34c © LOOK Die Bildagentur der Fotografen GmbH/Alamy; 35l AA/J Tims; 35c AA/C Sawyer; 35r AA/P Bennett; 47l AA/P Bennett; 47c AA/C Sawyer; 47r AA/J Tims; 48 © ALANDAWSONPHOTOGRAPHY/Alamy; 50c AA/P Bennett; 50b © Ian Shaw/Alamy; 51 © imagebroker/Alamy; 52/53 © Alberto Paredes/Alamy; 53 AA/P Bennett; 54 AA/P Bennett; 55t © ALANDAWSONPHOTOGRAPHY/Alamy; 55b © Alberto Paredes/Alamy; 56 AA/J Tims; 57 AA/P Bennett; 58 AA/P Bennett; 59 AA/P Bennett; 60 AA/P Bennett; 61 AA/M Chaplow; 62 AA/P Bennett; 63 AA/P Bennett; 64 AA/P Bennett; 65 AA/P Bennett; 73l AA/C Sawyer; 73c AA/M Chaplow; 73r AA/T Souter; 74 AA/P Bennett; 75 © PCL/Alamy; 76c AA/P Bennett; 76b Corbis; 77t AA/P Bennett; 77b © ALANDAWSONPHOTOGRAPHY/Alamy; 78/79 Adina Tovy Amsel/Eye Ubiquitous; 79t AA/N Setchfield; 79c AA/R Rainford; 80 Photolibrary Group; 81 AA/J Tims; 82 AA/J Tims; 83 AA/C Sawyer; 84 AA/P Bennett; 85 AA/P Bennett; 86/87 AA/J Tims; 87 AA/P Bennett; 88 AA/J Tims; 89 AA/C Sawyer; 90 AA/P Bennett; 91 AA/C Sawyer; 92 AA/C Sawyer; 93 AA/P Bennett; 94/95 AA/J Tims; 96 AA/J Tims; 101l The Travel Library; 101c AA/P Enticknap; 101r AA/P Bennett; 102 AA/J Tims; 104c AA/J Tims; 104b AA/P Bennett; 105 AA/C Sawyer; 106 AA/J Tims; 107 AA/J Tims; 108 AA/C Sawyer; 109 AA/P Bennett; 110 AA/C Sawyer; 111 AA/C Sawyer; 112 AA/P Bennett; 113 AA/P Bennett; 114 Pictures Colour Library; 115 © LOOK Die Bildagentur der Fotografen GmbH/Alamy; 116 © LOOK Die Bildagentur der Fotografen GmbH/ Alamy; 119l © PCL/Alamy; 119c AA/K Paterson; 119r AA/R Strange; 120 AA/J Tims; 121 © Maximilian Weinzierl/Alamy; 122 AA/C Sawyer; 123t AA/J Tims; 123b Photodisc; 124/125 AA/P Bennett; 125 © Eddie Gerald/Alamy; 126 AA/P Bennett; 127 AA/P Bennett; 128 © Peter Treanor/Alamy; 129 AA/C Sawyer; 130/131 AA/J Tims; 132 AA/P Bennett; 132/133 © Steffen Hauser/botanikfoto/ Alamy; 133 AA/P Bennett; 134 AA/C Sawyer; 135 AA/C Sawyer; 136 AA/C Sawyer; 136/137 © Maximilian Weinzierl/Alamy; 138 AA/P Bennett; 139 AA/C Sawyer; 140 AA/J Tims; 141 AA/C Sawyer; 142 AA/J Tims; 151l © Medio Images/ImageState; 151c AA/P Bennett; 151r AA/J Tims; 152 © Islandstock/Alamy; 154 © Ian Shaw/Alamy; 155l AA/P Bennett; 155r AA/P Bennett; 156 AA/P Bennett; 157 AA/P Bennett; 158 © Jon Arnold Images Ltd/Alamy; 160 AA/P Bennett; 161 AA/P Bennett; 162 AA/P Bennett; 163 AA/C Sawyer; 164 AA/J Tims; 165 AA/C Sawyer; 166 AA/C Sawyer; 167 AA/C Sawyer; 168 AA/P Bennett; 169l AA/P Bennett; 169c AA/P Bennett; 169r AA/A Mockford & N Bonetti; 173t AA/P Bennett; 173bl AA/J Tims; 173br AA/J Tims.

Every effort has been made to trace the copyright holders, and we apologise in advance for any accidental errors. We would be happy to apply any corrections in the following edition of this publication.

SPIRALGUIDE
Questionnaire

Dear Traveller

Your comments, opinions and recommendations are very important to us. Please help us to improve our travel guides by taking a few minutes to complete this simple questionnaire.

You do not need a stamp (unless posted outside the UK). If you do not want to remove this page from your guide, then photocopy it or write your answers on a plain sheet of paper.

Send to: The Editor, Spiral Guides, AA World Travel Guides, FREEPOST SCE 4598, Basingstoke RG21 4GY.

Your recommendations...

We always encourage readers' recommendations for restaurants, night-life or shopping – if your recommendation is used in the next edition of the guide, we will send you a FREE AA Spiral Guide of your choice. Please state below the establishment name, location and your reasons for recommending it.

_____

_____

_____

_____

_____

Please send me AA Spiral _____
(see list of titles inside the back cover)

About this guide...

Which title did you buy?

_____ **AA Spiral**

Where did you buy it?_____

When? m m / y y

Why did you choose an AA Spiral Guide? _____

_____

_____

_____

_____

Did this guide meet your expectations?

Exceeded ☐   Met all ☐   Met most ☐   Fell below ☐

Please give your reasons _____

_____

_____

_____

_____

continued on next page...

Were there any aspects of this guide that you particularly liked?

_____

_____

_____

_____

_____

Is there anything we could have done better?

_____

_____

_____

_____

About you...

Name (Mr/Mrs/Ms) _____

Address _____

_____

_____ **Postcode** _____

Daytime tel no _____ **email** _____

Please _only_ give us your email address and mobile phone number if you wish to hear from us about other products and services from the AA and partners by email or text or mms.

Which age group are you in?

Under 25 ☐   25–34 ☐   35–44 ☐   45–54 ☐   55–64 ☐   65+ ☐

How many trips do you make a year?

Less than one ☐   One ☐   Two ☐   Three or more ☐

Are you an AA member? Yes ☐   No ☐

About your trip...

When did you book? m m / y y   **When did you travel?** m m / y y

How long did you stay? _____

Was it for business or leisure? _____

Did you buy any other travel guides for your trip? ☐ Yes ☐ No

If yes, which ones? _____

_____

Thank you for taking the time to complete this questionnaire. Please send it to us as soon as possible, and remember, you do not need a stamp (unless posted outside the UK).
